SERVICE WITHOUT GUNS

Selected Books by the Authors

Donald J. Eberly, *A Profile of National Service*, 1966

Michael W. Sherraden and Donald J. Eberly, *National Service: Social, Economic and Military Impacts*, 1982

Reuven Gal, *Portrait of the Israeli Soldier*, 1986

Donald J. Eberly, *National Service: A Promise to Keep*, 1988

Reuven Gal and Thomas C. Wyatt, *Legitimacy and Commitment in the Military*, 1990

Donald Eberly and Michael Sherraden, *The Moral Equivalent of War? A Study of Non-Military Service in Nine Nations*, 1990

Reuven Gal and A. D. Mangelsdorff, *Handbook of Military Psychology*, 1991

Donald J. Eberly, *National Youth Service in the 20th and 21st Centuries*, 1997

SERVICE WITHOUT GUNS

Donald J. Eberly and Reuven Gal

With a guest chapter by Michael Sherraden

First published in 2006 by Donald J. Eberly and Reuven Gal

Printed in the United States of America

ISBN 1-4116-7283-6

Grateful acknowledgement is made to the following for permission to re-print previously published material:

Voluntary Action: The Journal of the Institute for Volunteering Research, London, Volume 5, No. 2, Spring 2003. "National Youth Service as an In-strument of Peace and Reconciliation," by Donald J. Eberly

The Responsive Community. Summer, 2004. "From Military Officer Cadets to NYS Volunteer Cadets: The Transformation from Military to Civic Service," by Donald J. Eberly and Reuven Gal

PREFACE

In December 2000, Reuven Gal sent Donald Eberly an e-mail inviting him to present a paper at the forthcoming conference of the Inter-University Seminar on Armed Forces and Society. The paper was to deal with linkages between military service and National Youth Service in the 20th Century. Eberly replied to say that he could not attend but suggested that it was a very important topic and we should write a book about it. That is how this book was born.

Interwoven as our respective backgrounds are with civilian service and military service and with research and work in a number of countries worldwide, the decision to proceed with this book is perhaps not surprising.

As an undergraduate at the Massachusetts Institute of Technology in the late 1940s, Donald Eberly was active in a student-led project that brought several hundred young men and women to MIT from countries that had been devastated by World War II and from developing countries for a summer of study and research. Today, Eberly and his colleagues would be called volunteers in a service-learning program. He served in the US Army as a draftee from 1951 to 1953 and later that year he went to teach physics and mathematics at Molusi College, Ijebu-Igbo, Nigeria. He left in 1956 and a few years later a Peace Corps Volunteer would occupy that position.

Eberly first circulated his proposal for National Youth Service (NYS), called "A National Service for Peace" in 1957. That led to the remainder of his career being devoted to NYS. Over the years, he has convened several conferences on NYS, testified before the US Congress and Canadian parliament on NYS, developed a plan for NYS at the request of a Presidential Commission in the US, conducted a number of research studies, managed a NYS test project, written numerous articles about NYS, and visited NYS projects in North and South

America, Central America and the Caribbean, Africa and Europe, the Middle East and Far East, and Australasia and the Pacific Islands.

Eberly was the founder and Director of the National Service Secretariat in the USA from 1966-1994 and became the Honorary President of the International Association for National Youth Service in 1998. He is the author of *National Service: A Promise to Keep*, 1988; the editor of *A Profile of National Service*, 1966; and the co-editor with Michael W. Sherraden of *National Service: Social, Economic and Military Impacts*, 1982, and of *The Moral Equivalent of War: A Study of Non-Military Service in Nine Nations*, 1990. Eberly moved to New Zealand in 1994.

As a boy, Reuven Gal was an active member and a "Madrich" (group-leader) in the Israeli Scouts Movement. He served in the Israeli Defense Forces (IDF) as a combat infantry officer from 1960-1963 and commanded a reserve reconnaissance unit during the battles in Jerusalem in the Six-Days War. After completing his academic studies in psychology and sociology with a B.A, and M.A. from the Hebrew University in Jerusalem and a Ph.D. from the University of California, Berkeley, Reuven served as IDF's Chief Psychologist from 1976-1982 and retired from the IDF with the rank of Colonel.

In 1985 Gal founded and subsequently headed the Carmel Institute for Social Studies, a non-profit research and policy-making center, which studies and promotes social and psychological projects, both in Israel and internationally. Among these projects is the Helping-the-Helpers program, designed to help mental-health professionals in the former-Yugoslav countries throughout their civil wars from 1992-2001. Similarly, he engaged in conflict-resolution and reconciliation issues in Northern Ireland, as well as in Jewish–Arab co-existence programs. In 1991 Gal, together with two colleagues, founded the Center for Outstanding Leadership in Zichron Ya'akov. In August 2002 he became the Deputy National Security Advisor for Domestic Policy at the Israeli

National Security Council, where he was in charge of promoting Sherut Leumi (NYS), a universal youth service.

Gal has attended numerous conferences on NYS and, as Deputy President of the International Association for National Youth Service, hosted its 2000 conference in Jerusalem. Besides his academic and research work (among his books are: *A Portrait of the Israeli Soldier*, 1986; *Legitimacy and Commitment in the Military*, 1990; *The Seventh War*, 1990, and *Handbook of Military Psychology*, 1991), Gal also serves as a senior consultant to Israel's National Memorial Museum and is a member of numerous other public and academic organizations.

Our experiences and studies and observations have led us to the conclusion that young people everywhere in the world would much rather cooperate with other young people in constructive activities than engage them in combat, and that the societies from which they come would much rather have the service of young people directed toward meeting basic human needs than toward domination of other societies by force of arms. We hope this book will contribute to many more young people having such constructive service opportunities.

*   *   *   *   *

This book was written from 2001 to 2005. Nearly all of the information resources come from the 20th Century. We generally refer to programs in the present tense if they were still in existence at the time of the writing and in the past tense if they were not.

With young people in NYS variously known as Volunteers, Corpers, Zivis, and (on rare occasions) Conscientious Objectors, we wanted a generic term that had more life to it than the usual "participants." We have taken the liberty of referring to young men and women in NYS as "cadets," carrying with it a connotation of youthfulness as well as work combined with learning. In New Zealand, a cadet is a young man who lives and works on a sheep station, learning the trade. In Israel, cadets are young trainees in leadership programs. NYS cadets are, indeed, young, committed and eager to learn.

We thank the thousands of NYS cadets we have met for the work they have done and for the insights into NYS that we have gained from them. We thank our fellow members of the International Association for National Youth Service for a substantial amount of information in this book and for the perspectives on NYS that they have shared with us. We salute persons we have known for the pioneering work they have done in developing and advancing NYS; persons such as Tai Solarin of Nigeria and Peter Kpordugbe of Ghana, Alec Dickson and Elisabeth Hoodless of the UK, Koesnadi Hardjasoemantri of Indonesia, Ali Raza Khan of Pakistan, Maria Nieves Tapia of Argentina, Jacques Hebert of Canada, Nicole Fleischer of Israel, and Eleanor Roosevelt, Hubert Humphrey, Morris Janowitz, Margaret Mead, Harris Wofford, Willard Wirtz, Charles Moskos, James Kielsmeier and Susan Stroud of the United States.

Special thanks go to Michael Sherraden, Benjamin E. Youngdahl Professor of Social Development and Director, Center for Social Development, Washington University in St. Louis. In addition to his authorship of Chapter 8, we are also grateful for his wise counsel over the years and his initiatives in advancing NYS.

Finally, we wish to thank Sheila Allison of Australia's University of Tasmania for offering to set up a web site and her colleague Anne Hugo for creating the web site (http://www.acys.utas.edu.au/ianys/) of the International Association for NYS in 1996, and for maintaining it since then; Nik Hollander and Sarah Hollander of New Zealand for invaluable computer advice and assistance; and Henning Sorenson of Denmark for suggesting the title, *Service without Guns*.

CONTENTS

INTRODUCTION

We have written this book because we believe the world will be a better place if civilian service by young people becomes as widespread and important in the 21st Century as military service was in the 20th Century.

If we can suggest how to get from here to there, from a world in which military activities have been in the forefront of the news almost every day in the last century, to a world in which everyone will know some young people in civilian service and be familiar with the work they do, perhaps this transformation will be a little more likely to happen.

Ever since the French Revolution over 200 years ago brought on the levee en masse of military forces, military service has been generally perceived as an obligation of young adult male citizens.   With exceptions for the physically disabled, the mentally retarded and mentally ill, convicted criminals, and Conscientious Objectors, everyone was expected to serve when called upon to do so.

Some young people in military service felt a sense of sacrifice and commitment, especially during times when they were part of a struggle for freedom, or when their country was threatened.   Many young people were eager to serve and volunteered before they were called into service.   They entered out of a sense of patriotism or adventure, or occasionally they enlisted in the Navy or Air Force to escape what they perceived as the harsher service they would encounter in the Army if they waited to be drafted.   Some volunteered for service to get away from one's home or community, to engage in something heroic, or even to increase one's chances of attracting the opposite sex.   Very likely in most cases, it was a combination of some or all of these factors that led young men to volunteer.   An unspoken cause of volunteering was an inherent sense that serving would offer them a rite of passage from adolescence to manhood.

Required military service was the brunt of a great deal of humor both from those in and out of service. Soldiers were unhappy when they were assigned to mess duty; they grumbled about long route marches; they whispered to one another about officers' stupidity as they "hurried up and waited." But anguish and tears replaced humor when conflicts left battlefields strewn with casualties.

The public and the politicians viewed military service as something that was necessary and that justified the expenditure of large amounts of taxpayer's money. Opposition numbers were very small, consisting primarily of persons conscientiously opposed to war and military service, and of civil libertarians.

Large-scale national civilian service by young people in the 20th Century achieved the kind of public recognition and acceptance accorded military service in very few countries, most notably in China, Israel, and Nigeria. Each of these nations had challenging military battles in the middle third of the century. China fought a revolution, Israel defended itself against a ferocious attack from its neighbors just a few days after gaining independence, and Nigeria fought a civil war. For the remainder of the century, each of these countries continued to accord high priority to service by young people, in both military and in civilian capacities.

We believe it is possible for countries to move steadily toward the adoption of large-scale civilian service without having to go through war and revolution. We perceive that recent trends in the family system, the use of computers, the view of the marketplace, and the striving for improved standards of living and a better environment have led to increased societal needs. We believe that the demand for those needs will continue to grow and lead to increased domestic and international strife. We know that young people in civic service can help to meet those needs and reduce the likelihood of strife.

Since the 1960s, the extended family system and the nuclear family system have suffered substantial erosion. The result is that the care of needy members of the family -- especially young children and old folks – has been left to others, whether paid or unpaid. Often that care is inferior to what it had been, and sometimes it is not there at all.

Since the 1970s, the revolution in computers and telecommunications has changed almost everything, from workplace activities to life in the home. This revolution has greatly reduced the amount of time required for many tasks at work and at home. However, it has not reduced the time needed to nurture a child or care for an old person, any more than it has reduced the time for an orchestra to play a symphony. Consequently, it has become relatively more expensive to attend concerts and to care for those in need.

Since the 1980s, many people have come to believe that the marketplace, where money is exchanged for goods and services, should be the sole determinant of society's priorities, human as well as material. A number of governments have acted on this idea by reducing the level of expenditures for those in need. Instead of providing public employment and health care, for example, many governments are leaving it up to the individual, with the result that the poorest people may spend what little money they have in attempts to escape their misery with alcohol and drugs rather than on food and medical care. More services to the needy are required.

Throughout the 20th Century, from radio to television to the Internet, people everywhere moved from relative ignorance of developments in other countries to a daily updating of developments. More than ever before, people everywhere aspire to better standards of living. Many hope simply for adequate food, clothing and shelter. Some focus on better health and education. Some of the most privileged persons in the world campaign for clean air and water and good recreational areas.

The result of these four powerful trends is that the most deprived and at-risk members of society are being neglected, while at the same time other sectors look for enriched services. The need for civilian service is greater than ever before.

At the same time that provision of services to those most in need of them is diminishing, we see in every country a proportion of young people who are on the fast track to education, careers, leadership and prosperity. They seem to live in a different world from another proportion of young people – usually a much larger one – who are on the road to lives of drudgery or unemployment, or perhaps looking to crime as the only way out.

Whichever world young people are in, they like to do new things and take risks. We see evidence of that in everyday life as young people experiment with dangerous drugs, consume too much alcohol, and drive dangerously on our roads. But they also want to participate, to be contributing members of society. However, society holds them back as it thinks they have not yet matured sufficiently to participate responsibly. What society fails to realize is that children do not gradually become adults. As they reach adolescence, they alternate between the role of children and the role of adults. When they feel childlike, they want the comfort of a parent. When they feel like adults, they want to be treated as adults, not as children. As they move through the teenage years, they spend more of their time in an adult role and less in that of a child.

Shouldn't we look for ways that permit young people to alternate these roles, where we trust them to do important work while having support readily at hand? Shouldn't we give them the opportunity to engage their sense of adventure while serving others? The situation is somewhat analogous to that in military service, where young people encounter challenges, do important work, and have support readily available. But would it be possible to find another primary cause, other than wars, that might come to be viewed as the moral equivalent of military service? Is there a way in which young people can have experiences analogous to those of soldiers in wartime, with plenty of challenges and hard work, but without the violence and destruction?

We believe there is, and we suggest that a substantial part of the answer can be found in the relatively new forms of service known as National Youth Service and the closely related service-learning. National Youth Service is a mechanism by which the needs that exist in every country can be joined with the resource represented by young people from all walks of life. If it were possible to measure the totality of benefits of NYS, it is likely that the benefits to the NYS cadets would exceed the benefits to the persons served by a substantial margin. The NYS experience often sets the course for the remainder of one's life.

We have taken as the definition of National Youth Service that used by the International Association for National Youth Service, namely: "National Youth Service (NYS) is an organized activity in which young people serve others and the environment in ways that contribute positively to society. NYS participants have opportunities for reflection, normally serve full-time for six months to two years, and receive support – whether from government or NGOs – sufficient to enable them to serve. NYS also embraces service-learning, where students utilize their education to serve others and where students reflect on their service experiences to inform their learning."

This book is comprised of four parts; namely, Military Service at the Beginning of the 21st Century, What is National Youth Service all about? The Impact of NYS, and The Future of NYS. Also, many of the chapters contain brief vignettes of NYS in action around the world.

The opportunity to move from large-scale military service to large-scale NYS comes in part from the steady reduction in the size of the armed forces in many countries, as described in Chapter 1. Given the strength and array of benefits received by NYS cadets, one would think that NYS would emerge as a consequence of youth development policy. Paradoxically, however, we see in Chapters 2 and 3 that NYS programs generally come about for other reasons. The problem seems to be that when youth policy officials design a program of youth development, they do it as a reaction to perceived youth problems such as alcohol and drug abuse, accidental pregnancies, and unemployment. Then they create a program that does things to young people, such as telling them the evils of alcohol and drugs, showing them how to prevent pregnancy, and training them in various skills. The youth policy officials are often baffled when these measures fail to make a significant dent in perceived youth problems.

Once the public and politicians realize that young people should not be regarded as problems but as people who have a lot of potential and who want to participate actively and constructively in society, we believe they will see the value of challenging them to contribute to society and of supporting them in making a contribution. Many officials will then be surprised to see that the objectives they were hoping to achieve by doing things to young people are better met by challenging them to serve in NYS along the lines described in Chapter 4.

A major outcome of NYS programs is the learning acquired by the NYS cadets. That learning can be enhanced by incorporating the principles of service-learning into NYS programs. Although service-learning programs usually engage students in part-time service, we view the service-learning process as an integral part of NYS, one which can be applied to cadets in full-time service. Chapter 5 describes examples of service-learning, its outcomes, and a model design for a service-learning program. Many forms of learning are found in the service-learning process, ranging from history lessons acquired by talking with old people in a nursing home to gaining a sense of one's career options.

Participation in NYS activities benefits the cadets no less than the needy. Besides skills acquisition, learning to work in teams and in the adult world, and preparing for employment and higher education, NYS also has significant psychological and developmental aspects. The range of social and psychological outcomes to be gleaned from NYS is explored in Chapter 6.

What is the impact of NYS? Is it different in different parts of the world? Studies from various parts cited in Chapter 7 suggest a surprising degree of common outcomes, both in regard to the service performed and the impact on cadets.

The multiplicity of benefits that can be expected from well-run NYS programs suggest that NYS is properly viewed as "strong policy," a theme developed in Chapter 8 by our guest contributor and colleague Michael Sherraden.

The events of the first few years of the 21st Century remind us that war, terrorism, and conflicts are unlikely to disappear anytime soon; neither are we immune from natural disasters. Chapter 9 explains the kinds of roles that NYS cadets can play in post-war and post-disaster reconstruction.

A practical question posed by anyone keen on advancing NYS is "How do we do it?" Although it is not going to happen overnight, numerous avenues can followed in advancing NYS. They are given in Chapter 10.

In conclusion, Chapter 11 summarizes the likely outcomes for countries that adopt NYS programs and suggests possible conceptual frameworks for viewing NYS.

*   *   *   *   *

In a number of countries in the 20th Century, military service was referred to as national service. It was seen as service to the nation. The nation financed the military because it was seen to be in the national interest. The public accepted military service as a responsibility of citizenship. In this century, we believe that NYS has the potential to become at least as much in the national interest, and as much a responsibility of citizenship, as military service was in the last century.

As young people, both of us served in the military forces of our respective countries and both of us engaged in NYS-type activities, although not in formal NYS programs. From our experiences as young people and our first-hand knowledge of NYS activities in many parts of the world, we know that – like military service – young people in NYS often face greater challenges, shoulder more responsibility, and learn more about themselves than they have ever done before. We suggest that young people as well as families, communities, educational institutions, and nations will have a better future if they consider the kind of NYS that is best for them and act on their conclusions.

PART I

INTER-RELATIONSHIP OF MILITARY SERVICE AND CIVIC SERVICE

While the number of young people in military service was on the decline in the latter part of the 20th Century, a number of military service features can be found in forms of civic service that have developed in various parts of the world.

CHAPTER 1

MILITARY SERVICE AT THE BEGINNING OF THE 21ST CENTURY

The first responsibility of states – as it was to the clans and tribes and fiefdoms that preceded them – is the protection of their people, whether from wild animals or invading armies. For thousands of years, societies have mobilized their young men, trained them, and equipped them with the weapons of the time. During the latter half of the 20th Century, rapid advances in technology as well as massive political changes have permitted countries to reduce the size of their armies while increasing their fire-power.

Transitions and Transformations in Military Organizations

In a historical perspective, the 'military model' is ever-changing and transforming; it is a function of technology, the changing environment, and political situations.

Charles Moskos, among other scholars in military sociology, claims that even within the last century, military organizations have undergone, in almost all states and countries, a major common transition (Moskos, 2000). This transition can be captured in various characteristics, or "armed-forces variables", ranging from the force structure to its approach toward homosexuals and conscientious objectors. This multi-dimensional transition is neatly portrayed in Table 1 (opposite page).

Thus, the postmodern military is characterized by diminishing support from the public. Also, its orientation and ethos are more tolerant and flexible, making it less distinct

Table 1: Armed Forces Transitions in the 20th Century

Armed Forces Variable	**Modern** (Pre-Cold War) 1900-1945	**Late Modern** (Cold War) 1945-1990	**Postmodern** (Post-Cold War) Since 1990
Perceived Threat	Enemy invasion	Nuclear war	Subnational (e.g., ethnic violence, terrorism)
Force Structure	Mass army, conscription	Large professional army	Small professional (voluntary) army
Major Mission Definition	Defense of homeland	Support of alliance	New missions (e.g., peacekeeping, humanitarian)
Dominant Military Professional	Combat leader	Manager or technician	Soldier-statesman; soldier-scholar
Public Attitude toward Military	Supportive	Ambivalent	Skeptical or apathetic
Media Relations	Incorporated	Manipulated	Courted
Civilian Employees	Minor component	Medium component	Major component
Women's Role	Separate corps or excluded	Partial integration	Full integration
Spouse and Military	Integral part	Partial involvement	Removed
Homosexuals in Military	Punished	Discharged	Accepted
Conscientious Objection	Limited or prohibited	Routinely permitted	Subsumed under civilian services

Source: Moskos et.al, 2000.

from civil society than it was in the past; and the motivation of the servicemen (and women!) is not necessarily patriotic, but rather stems from the desire for self-actualization and exposure to occupational opportunities.

The emergence of the postmodern army stems, obviously, from the end of the Cold War and the collapse of the

Soviet block and the Warsaw Pact. It is also the result of vast economic, cultural and societal changes occurring in the West, including "globalization," the weakening of the nation-state, the increase in standards-of-living, changes in the workplace, and the erosion of traditional values (Haltiner, 1998; Von Bredow, 1999; Moskos et.al, 2000;).

But perhaps the most striking transformation (and the most relevant to the present discussion) is the decline, almost disappearance, of the universal (mandatory or compulsory) conscription-based army. The conscript ratios – the share of conscripts as a percentage of armed forces strength – in Figures 1 and 2 show the pronounced shift away from conscription and toward All-Volunteer Forces. Figure 1 (page 13) shows that among 19 European countries in 2005, only two had maintained or increased their conscript ratios, compared to the Cold War era. In the same 19 countries from 1991 to 2004, the number of persons serving in the armed forces declined from 13 million to 6 million (Haltiner & Tresch, 2005).

Figure 2 (page 14) shows that as of 2005, the only countries left in Europe that still maintained "hard-core" conscript forces were Greece, Turkey, Finland and Switzerland.[1] Starting in the early Sixties and up until 2005, all other North American and European countries had transformed their militaries into all-volunteer forces (AVF's), or were in the process of doing so.

Furthermore, the overall participation ratio of persons in military service out of the entire population, among 15 Western European countries, had diminished from around 5% in the 1970's and 80's – to less than 3%, in 2000 (Haltiner, 2001). In several countries, notably Germany, France, Great Britain and Holland – this percentage is below 0.5% (The Military Balance, 2000).

---

[1] It should be noted that Israel, too, is still maintaining a full mandatory service within this sample of Western Democratic states.

Figure 1: Conscript Ratios: 1975-1989 to 2005 (19 nations*)*

Key: 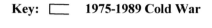 1975-1989 Cold War

◀ 2005

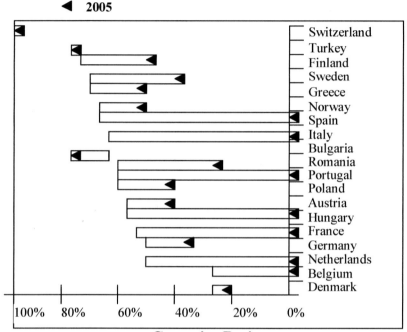

Conscript Ratios

Source: Haltiner & Tresch, 2005

Although there are a number of exceptions, due largely to a perceived need for increased military prepared-ness, this dual process of down-sizing in strength and trans-forming in structure from conscription to all-voluntary forces can also be found in countries in Asia and Africa. For exam-ple, the Thailand Armed Forces had reached 70 percent of its recruitment from volunteers in 2001 (Bangkok Post, 2001), thus putting this country in the Type 1 (Conscript Ratio be-low 50%) category of Karl Haltiner's typology. A similar trend is taking place in India (AAIW, 2002).

Recent transformations of military organizations, however, apply not only to their size and structure, but also to their mission and orientation. Along with an increasing tendency to engage in peace-keeping and constabulary missions (rather than in all-out-war actions), many military organizations have become involved in domestic and humanitarian

Figure 2: Conscript Ratios (CR) in the European Armed Forces – A Typology (2005/06)

All Volunteer Forces Type 0 (No conscripts)	Pseudo Conscript Forces Type I (CR < 50%)	Soft Core Conscript Forces Type II (CR < 50-66%)	Hard Core Conscript Forces Type III (CR > 66%)
▽	▽	▽	▽
United Kingdom Ireland Luxemburg Belgium (1992) Netherlands (1996) France (2003) Portugal (2004) Hungary (2004) Slovenia (2004) Italy (2005) Spain (2005) Czech Rep. (2005) Slovakia (2006) Denmark (2006)	Austria Germany Latvia Lithuania Norway Russia Serbia Sweden	Bulgaria Croatia Estonia Poland Romania	Finland Greece Switzerland Turkey

Source: Haltiner & Tresch, 2005

missions (or, as the military jargon refers to it, 'Military Operations Other Then War' – MOOTW). Such missions include rescue operations, fire-fighting, helping uprooted populations in refugee camps, and food supply.

This trend of "Military Humanitarianism" (Weiss & Campbell, 1991), brings the military service as close as ever to the civic-service model, which includes all kinds of operations <u>but</u> war, or -- in William James' term (see Chapter 2) -- bears the title "moral equivalent of war" (James, 1910).

*   *   *   *   *

These transitions and transformations of military organizations, which occurred throughout the last decades of the 20th Century, have been major factors in the growth of civic service during these same decades. As armies shrink in size and move toward non-military missions, more young people are available for organizations that are more civilian in the first place. Although the linkage between the numbers of people in military and civic service is seldom one of inverse proportionality, the trend toward smaller, more professional armies does increase the pool of young people available for civic service initiatives.

CHAPTER 2

LINKAGES BETWEEN CIVIC AND MILITARY SERVICE IN THE 20TH CENTURY

This chapter examines the development of various modes of civic service during the 20th Century in the five countries that have had the most substantial efforts; namely, the United States, Germany, China, Israel, and Nigeria. It is worth noting that although they are in various parts of the world, in each of these countries there have been significant linkages between civic and military service.

Throughout history the dividing line between military and civic service has not been as clear-cut as their names would imply. Nubian soldiers in the army of Old Egypt built monuments that still stand. The Incan Army in South America built roads and irrigation systems. The soldiers of Etruria built aqueducts around Rome to supply water to the city. And later the Roman Army built Hadrian's wall and highways, some of which form the motorways of today's England. (Glick, 1967: 33)

More recent years have seen the arrangement whereby civilian service has become a recognized alternative to required military service. Prior to independence in 1776, most of the American colonies introduced this feature (Chambers, 1993:). And in 1787, Catherine the Great of Russia gave Mennonite Conscientious Objectors freedom from military service in exchange for working for four years with fire brigades or the forestry department. (Ponomarenko, 2001).

Although the idea for translating the non-lethal features of military service into constructive activities goes back at least as far as Isaiah's prophecy that people "shall beat their swords into plowshares and their spears into pruninghooks," the development of the concept that is generally referred to as National Youth Service (NYS) has been largely a 20th Century phenomenon.

United States

It was Harvard University Professor William James who set forth the conceptual framework for NYS. While a visiting professor at Stanford University in 1906 he gave a major address to the university community entitled "The Moral Equivalent of War." He called for "a conscription of the whole youthful population to work on many of the toughest jobs." They would go "to coal and iron mines, to freight trains, to fishing fleets in December, to dish-washing, clothes-washing, and window-washing, to road–building and tunnel-making, to foundries and stokeholes...." Those who served "would have paid their blood-tax, done their own part in the immemorial human warfare against nature; they would tread the earth more proudly, the women would value them more highly, they would be better fathers and teachers of the following generation." (James, 1968: 669.)

Although James placed himself "squarely in the anti-militarist camp," he said that martial values such as "intrepidity, contempt of softness, and surrender of private interest" must be the enduring cement of society. And he noted that painful work would be "done cheerily because the duty is temporary and threatens not, as now, to degrade the whole remainder of one's life." (James, 1968: 668-669.)

William James was a professor at Harvard when Franklin D. Roosevelt was a student there. But no record has yet come to light in which Roosevelt credits James for the inspiration behind America's largest, and probably most successful NYS program, the Civilian Conservation Corps (CCC). One of Roosevelt's first acts as President in 1933 was to oversee the creation of the CCC, whose declared purposes were to do important conservation work, to alleviate a very high level of youth unemployment, and to transfer money to very poor families. Most of the cadets' monthly pay was sent directly to their families, some of whom were on the brink of starvation.

The CCC met its goals. From 1933 until its wartime demise in 1942, an average of 300,000 young men were at work in the CCC at any one time. That figure represents about 30 percent of the age cohort of young men. The value of the work they did in projects such as planting billions of trees, building thousands of bridges and over 100,000 miles of minor roads, has been estimated at many times total program costs. (Sherraden and Eberly, 1982) And the transfer of money to the families was a godsend to them as there was not the safety net of social security and welfare that came later.

Not only was the CCC in keeping with James's design and outcomes, it was dependent on the US army for its basic administration. The CCC camps were run by military officers. Corps members got up to morning reveille, were assigned to mess duty, and performed daily drills -- without guns. Only their work projects were supervised by civilian officials. And the CCC had an unexpected impact on the military. Many of its former members entered military service early in World War II and adapted easily to the military lifestyle because of their experience in the CCC.

Following World War II, America learned one important lesson from the GI Bill, but failed to learn a second. The GI Bill provided higher education and training for one half of the 15 million persons who had served in the war, although officials had estimated that not more than one million veterans would take advantage of the GI Bill. That convinced the nation that Federal assistance for higher education was a good idea and the Congress passed legislation providing that assistance. But the nation overlooked the value of the service experience to those who took up the GI Bill. During their service period of several years, many were exposed to occupations they never would have considered had they stayed home.

Some worked on radar installations. Others learned foreign languages. Many had seen cultures far different from their own. In short, the service experience had whetted their educational appetites and had given them an experiential foundation for their further studies.

During the 1960 Presidential campaign, John F. Kennedy received enthusiastic support from university campuses for his proposed Peace Corps. Much of that support was because Kennedy had said he would consider making Peace Corps service an alternative to what was then a required military service. (Michigan State News, 1961). However, he backed away from that idea because he felt the draft was too hot an issue. One consequence was that among local draft boards – which operated with considerable autonomy – some excempted Peace Corps Volunteers from military service, others deferred them until they returned home, and still others drafted them while still in the Peace Corps.

The draft was a much hotter issue in 1966 when a conference of educators, government officials, and NGO representatives reignited the call for civic service. The New York Times endorsed the conference's proposed option plan and editorialized: "Nationally sound reform lies in the direction of universal national service, with limited options to serve either in the armed forces, the Peace Corps, the National Teacher Corps or a variety of domestic urban and rural missions."(The New York Times, 1966).

Morris Janowitz, a leading military sociologist and founder of the Inter-University Seminar on Armed Forces and Society, called for a civic service that would serve as a bridge between the military and civilian sectors of society and noted, along with William James, that some jobs were better done by short-termers. He said "we are dealing with the inescapable fact that many operational tasks are better performed by persons who do not have trained incapacities. One way of organizing these work situations is to have persons perform them for short periods of time without having to confront the issue of a career in that particular vocation." (Janowitz, 1967).

In 1966, President Lyndon Johnson created a commission to examine both Selective Service and NYS. He said he wanted to develop "a manpower service program that could work at every level of society.... To the youth of America, I want to say: if you seek to be uncommon, if you seek to make a difference, if you seek to serve, then look around you. Your country needs you. Your Nation needs your services." (Johnson, 1966).

By the time Johnson's commission made its report in 1967, Johnson had decided to escalate the war in Vietnam and passed the word to the commission not to recommend NYS. The Commission followed the President's instruction, but it did commend the idea of NYS and suggested pilot projects to further test the idea. During the '70s and 80s, a number of such projects were carried out, supported variously by the federal, state, and local governments and by the private sector. Together with additional studies and subsequently the strong support of President Clinton, they led to the creation of AmeriCorps in 1993. Clinton did not get the multi-billion dollar budget for AmeriCorps that he sought, but the latest incarnation of NYS was launched and by 2002 reached an enrollment of some 40,000 young people at any one time. That is equal to about one percent of a single year cohort of young men and women.

Germany

Shortly before the outbreak of World War I, Eugen Rosenstock-Huessy of Germany called for a social service corps. He wrote to "the Prussian Ministry of War, saying there were so many one-and two-year recruits freed from military service for ridiculous reasons of health. They should all be collected together in a social service corps where they could practice living and learning how to live."(Rosenstock-Huessy, 1978). His proposal got nowhere immediately but later he did organize a variety of short-term service corps efforts. Rosenstock-Huessy said he learned two major lessons from these experiments. First, they were far more successful when they involved young people from different strata of society than those from a homogenous group. He was later to criticize the Civilian Conservation Corps in the USA for failing to heed that lesson. Second, he found that short-term work camps had little impact. "As war must be replaced by something as earnest or nearly as earnest, I must insist that it is necessary to sacrifice some period of time, a considerable period, a chapter of your life."(Rosenstock-Huessy, 1978b)

Rosenstock-Huessy left Germany in disgust in 1933 and emigrated to the USA where, as a professor at Harvard and Dartmouth, he was the guiding light in a successful effort to enroll a couple of dozen university students in the CCC together with some unemployed young men. Eleanor Roosevelt visited the project – named Camp William James -- and gave it her stamp of approval, but then the USA entered World War II and that was the end of it.

NYS returned to Germany some years after the war but in quite a different context. Germany's post-war constitution states: "No one shall be forced to do war service with arms against his conscience." (Kuhlmann and Likkert, 1993) This provision led to alternative service for conscientious objectors (COs) when conscription was re-introduced in the late 1950s. CO applicants had to appear before a panel and try to convince members that they were genuine COs. Only a handful of young men became COs and were assigned to their civic service activities through an organization called Zivildienst.

However, the number of cadets in Zivildienst gradually rose during the 1960s and the system of having to convince a panel of one's genuineness in expressing his conscientious objection to war service led to complaints that the system discriminated in favor of the well-educated who could better present their arguments. The argument won the day and in the 1970s, West Germany took a number of measures to correct the situation. By the early 1980s, a young man only had to sign a paper saying he was a CO. Then he was assigned to alternative civilian service instead of military service. That practice was found to be unconstitutional and was replaced by the young man writing to the induction board giving his reasons for his request for CO status, together with his resume and good conduct certificate from the police. About 85 percent of such requests were approved and by 2000 there were some 180,000 young men classified as COs who were either in Zivildienst or awaiting assignment to it. The period of civilian service is one-third longer than military service.

According to the Federal Ministry of Defense, the proportion of young men available for conscription who had become COs in 2000 was 38 percent, somewhat higher than the 30 percent going into military service at the time. Of the remaining 32 percent most were exempt because of physical or mental disabilities while a few were excused for professional or compassionate reasons. For comparison, two full-time volunteer service programs initially unrelated to military service – the Volunteer Social Year and the Volunteer Ecology Year -- enrolled about one percent of a single year cohort of young people. Since 90 percent are young women, that means that nearly two percent of young women enroll in one of them, a sharp contrast with the 38 percent in alternative civilian service.

There was also a dramatic shift in the public's view of civic service. As the number of young men performing civilian national service at any one time had risen from a few thousand in the 1960s to 130,000 in the mid-1980s, and as a larger percentage of the public had become familiar with the work of Zivildienst, the public attitude had shifted from negative -- viewing COs as deviants and draft-dodgers -- to positive. (Kuhlmann, 1990)

By the end of the century, Germany faced a dilemma. The Cold War had ended and the military manpower pool had increased as a result of the unification of West and East Germany. There was no longer a need for conscription. But the young men in civic service had become a vital part of the delivery of social services, especially to old people. (Kuhlmann and Lippert in Moskos, 1993) The government appeared to be stalling on moving toward an all-volunteer military force because Zivildienst would collapse along with it. One option under consideration was to create both a volunteer military and a volunteer civic service and encourage young men and women to choose one of these services.

China

China does not have to concern itself with conscription as there are always more than enough volunteers to fill the ranks. Its People's Liberation Army (PLA) is a good example of Mao Zedong's admonition to "serve the people." He intended that virtually everyone in China be occupied in a way that served the greater good of the Chinese people. Thus, his statement that "there is no profound difference between the farmer and the soldier" (Glick, 1967:41) might as easily be applied to the teacher or the fisherman or the factory worker. Such a broad definition of service complicates the task of identifying civic service activities as distinct from salaried employment.

Still, there can be little doubt that the young men of the PLA have provided an enormous amount of civilian service. In the second half of the 20th Century, the Chinese army constructed 8,000 miles of railway, planted hundreds of millions of trees, brought one million acres of land under irrigation, constructed 40 iron and steel factories and 20 coal mines, provided medical assistance and public health education to much of the population, and responded to thousands of natural disasters.

In China in 1978 I visited a Home for Respect of the Aged – a nursing home – and met a barefoot doctor. She had few supplies and limited skills but she was making a difference and clearly was appreciated by the residents. (DJE)

China also provides incentives for young people outside the military to do civic service kinds of activities. In a program called the Poverty Alleviation Relay Project (PARP), university graduates are asked to go to the countryside to teach school for a year or two. Doing so greatly increases their chances of obtaining an interesting job and decent housing on their return to the city.

Through the Chinese Young Volunteers Association (CYVA), established in 1994, young volunteers are individually linked with retired persons in a program known as "one-on-one." The All-China Youth Federation reported that in 1996 young volunteers, who number in the hundreds of thousands, were encouraged to contribute at least 48 hours of voluntary service each year.

The civilian activities of the young people in the PLA, in universities, and in the CYVA comprise only a fraction of the total service output by young Chinese. Additional activities are carried on in urban neighborhoods and rural areas, in labor units and factories, in primary and secondary schools, and by members of the Communist Youth League. Clearly the youth service activities in China are very substantial.

Israel

Chairman Mao's dictum that there is no difference between a farmer and a soldier also applies to Israel. Soon after its independence, the parliament passed a military service law declaring that "Agricultural training will be an integral part of military service."

While still under the British mandate and before the Jewish state was created in 1947, Jewish leaders had established various para-military groups and pioneer youth movements which they described to the British overlords as nothing more than Boy Scout troops. But much of the underlying rationale for these youth groups was to develop a cadre of young people who would be trained in military discipline, who could go on long route marches through the desert, and who would be ready to defend the nation state when the time came. With the birth of Israel and its frequent wars with its neighbors, Israel maintained a high state of readiness combined with development of the land.

Both young men and women are conscripted into the Armed Forces. As recently as the 1980s, more than 75 percent of Israeli young people did military service. But by 2000 the number had edged below 50 percent as the army became increasingly professionalized. The low participation rate concerned many Israelis who believed that service by young people was vital to national development, and who saw it as a rite of passage to adulthood. A number of civic service programs – called Sherut Leumi -- have developed over the years to meet this demand. One such example is Bat Ami, an NGO which recruits some 3,000 religious young women for a year or two of social service. Another 1,000 young women of varied beliefs serve in Shlomit, which by 2000 had expanded to include also a few Arabs and young men in their service projects. About the same number of women in the Army are assigned to civilian service activities, sometimes alongside those in Bat Ami and Shlomit.

Altogether, Sherut Leumi includes some 7,000 young people in full-time, year-round service. Since all but a few of them are women, that equals about 12 percent of the single year cohort of young women.

The proportion of young Israelis performing civic service would increase if a proposal made by Reuven Gal and others were adopted. The proposal is for a universal civic youth service of all Arab and Jewish citizens in Israel who, for whatever reasons, were not called into military service. A 1995 survey of Arab high school students revealed that 60 percent would readily enter such a Civic Youth Service. (Gal, 1995).

Nigeria

A slightly different form of a Civic Youth Service was established in Nigeria following the Civil War of the late 1960s when one part of Nigeria -- called Biafra -- tried to break away from the rest of Nigeria. The attempted breakaway can be traced directly to the fact that Nigeria is not a natural country.   Its borders were drawn by the European powers meeting in Berlin late in the 19th Century. They divided people of common language and culture, and they joined into one country people of different cultures.

Biafra failed in its effort to secede but Nigeria decided it must make efforts to foster national unity.   University students and other youth groups called for a national youth scheme whose first projects would be the provision of relief in war-torn areas. The Committee of Vice-Chancellors called for one year of service by all university students following their first year.   After much debate and considerable controversy, Head of State General Yakubu Gowon issued a decree in 1973 creating the National Youth Service Corps to develop "common ties among the youths of Nigerian and to promote national unity."

In Nigeria in 1962 I dropped in on a biology class in a high school in Benin being taught by a Peace Corps Volunteer. I was enthralled by his description of the disease kwashiorkor -- as were his students – and stayed for the whole class period.   Only a few teachers I had had over the years measured up to his standard.   In 2004 I dropped in on a high school geography class in Ikenne being taught by a member of the National Youth Service Corps (NYSC) and was equally impressed. I also met with 16 other NYSC cadets serving in the same area; all were from other parts of Nigeria, most were teachers, a few worked in village administration and one was a physician.   All were serving in the fields in which they received their university degrees. (DJE)

The NYSC requires all university graduates to serve for one year in a different part of the country from where they grew up. Until 2000, the army was responsible for overall administration at the national and state levels, while the cadet's immediate supervisor on the job was usually a civilian.   Following a quasi-military orientation period, they are posted to their places of assignment where they are expected not only to work for eleven months in a regular job, but also to initiate community development projects in the areas where they serve.

Cadets serve in their professional areas. Agricultural graduates advise farmers on crops and pesticides while English majors teach high school English. The government provides stipends for them. After service, cadets are brought together again to discuss their experiences, to participate in a passing out parade, and to receive a Certificate of National Service that entitles them to be employed in Nigeria. Although the posting of cadets to distant parts of Nigeria is not popular among entering members and their families, a study of ex-Corps members attitudes to being posted away from their home areas showed that in retrospect only one in ten were negative, the rest positive. (Enegwea, 1993) A summary of the account given by Alhaji Sani Garba, a recent Corps member, of a year in the NYSC portrays life in the community development aspect of NYSC.

After graduating from university, Garba received his call to NYS he was sad, as he viewed it as a year of suffering and hardship, and did not want to be deployed from the north to the southwest – it was a long way from his parents. Following his three-week-orientation, he was posted to a remote village with no transport, no electricity, no clean water, and poor sanitation. He had to stay and learn how to survive, because the assigned location could not be changed. Money was minimal, so he used his elementary school carpentry skills to build a bed, and make a mattress from the grasses. His demonstration of mattress-making inspired the whole village to make mattresses. As sanitation was poor, he worried he would get sick, so he built a pit latrine (there were no facilities prior to this). He also helped the villagers to dig mini-wells to find clean water. He said "The community learnt a lot from me and I learnt a lot from the community.... I went in a Northerner and came out a Nigerian." (Community Service Volunteers, 1998).

While nearly all university graduates serve in the NYSC – there are a few exemptions for age, entry into the army, etc. – the annual enrollment of some 130,000 comprises only about six percent of the single year cohort of young adults.

Conclusions

First, like military service, civic service can operate successfully on a large scale. There are any number of small programs that have been successful, perhaps because of a particularly-talented leader or an unique local situation, but that is not sufficient proof that they can function well on a large scale. We have seen successful large-scale service programs with the CCC in the USA, the People's Liberation Army of China, Zivildienst in Germany, Sherut Leumi in Israel, and the National Youth Service Corps in Nigeria.

Second, as with military service, if civic service is to attract a substantial proportion of young people, it should be consistent with the national ethos so that young people accept the rationale for service. Thus, service in China is seen as continuing the revolution of the mid 20th Century that got rid of despots and installed the new China. The ethos in Israel was initially the preservation of the nation by the military mobilization of virtually all young men and women; as military needs lessened, the ethos of universal service remained strong and young people not called for military service are expected to do civilian service. In Germany, equity considerations dictated that young men who did not do civilian service should do an equitable civilian service, and many young men find a period of civilian service to be a more agreeable option than a somewhat shorter period of military service. The German case is especially interesting because the number of young men choosing the civilian option is about the same as the number choosing the military option. One may hypothesize that the number choosing the military option would rise if Germany were threatened militarily while the number would fall if German soldiers were being sent to an unpopular war.

Third, civic and military service are by no means completely distinct from one another. From the Etruscans in millennia past to the Boxing Day tsunami of 2004, soldiers have provided a wide variety of civilian service. Although armies are getting smaller, they continue the millennia-old tradition of being assigned to civilian service projects. In 2000, Venezuela established Plan Bolivar that has soldiers building roads and schools as well as operating medical clinics. Beginning in 2003, Brazil announced plans to assign fairly substantial numbers of its 185,000 member military to activities ranging from road-building to recreation to assuming responsibility for procurement at the Ministry of Transportation. Also, many civic service programs employ military characteristics in their organization and training, as noted above with programs such as America's CCC and Nigeria's NYSC.

Fourth, similarities between military and civic service are also seen in areas such as teamwork, unit cohesion, and the joining together of young people from different walks of life in common cause. Furthermore, whether as soldiers or as NYS cadets, young people in service can be expected to perform well -- whether serving as volunteers or in compulsory service programs – as long as they accept the rationale for service. The Nigerian members of the NYSC who are teaching school perform at the same level as the salaried employees teaching in the same school. The German members of Zivildienst doing the same jobs as members of the Voluntary Social Year perform them just as well. In Chapters 4 and 6, we shall also note common outcomes of the service experience to those in different kinds of service.

Fifth, while civic service is at times comprised of persons who object to military service, as in Germany's Zivildienst and Israel's Bat Ami, at other times the two forms of service are complementary, as with the USA's AmeriCorps, Nigeria's NYSC, and China's PARP.

*   *   *   *   *

Thus, experiences with NYS in the 20th Century suggest that, in terms of the needs of individual countries, of society-at-large, and of young people the world over, NYS can successfully replace military service to a substantial extent. It could become in the 21st Century as much an institution of society as military service was in the 20th Century.

PART II

WHAT IS NATIONAL YOUTH SERVICE ALL ABOUT?

Although National Youth Service has different roots in different countries, a great deal is known about elements of program design and execution. Service-learning -- one of the elements – deserves its own chapter.

CHAPTER 3

TRENDS TOWARD NATIONAL YOUTH SERVICE

The gradual growth of NYS has been a multi-faceted process, stemming from various sources and involving diverse routes, sometimes as an alternative to military service, and at other times related to nation-building, education, employment, and service delivery. Also, the perception of volunteer service has expanded to include NYS; international service has grown, and certain regional trends have become discernible. Taken together, they appear to represent a trend toward the growth of NYS.

Alternative Civilian Service (ACS)

Performing civilian service as an alternative to required military service was rare until late in the 20th Century. Countries such as Russia, France and the United States occasionally permitted some form of alternative service on the basis of conscience, but it was granted not so much out of principle as expedience. Very small numbers of young men affiliated with minor religious sects were involved and states reckoned it would be easier to grant alternative service than to prosecute the offenders. In the USA in World War I, for example, there was no provision for alternative service for Conscientious Objectors (COs) and all 21,000 of those who were fit for military duty were placed in the armed forces. Most of them bowed to military pressure and accepted either combatant or non-combatant military assignments. There were still about 2,000 who refused any military order but did accept the military's proposal that they work on farms under civilian supervision. (Chambers, 1993)

During World War II, there were some 50,000 recognized COs in the USA, less than one percent of the 15 million who served in the Armed Forces. Most entered noncombatant military service, but some 12,000 were assigned to Civilian Public Service Camps run by the historic peace churches such as the Mennonites. The work they did was at least as hard as that envisioned by William James, as they served on conservation projects, in mental institutions, and as human guinea pigs for diseases such as malaria and typhus.

In recent decades, the increasing secularization of CO status has made it easier to become a CO. For example, in the United States until 1973 the local draft board checked on a person's religious affiliation and if he was a Mennonite, Quaker, or Brethren, that would be sufficient to justify classification as a CO. Young men from other religious denominations and atheists found it far more difficult to gain such a classification. Although the draft has not been in effect since 1973, rules introduced in the early 1980s would open the doors much more broadly to include atheists and men of other religious persuasion, and almost certainly including selective objectors, or those opposed only to what they consider unjust wars.

Pressure on the system of military conscription has also come from the increasing numbers of men seeking CO status. In the United States in the early 1970s, more young men sought CO status than were being drafted into the military services. In Germany in the 1980s and 1990s, over 100,000 men per year were serving in Zivildienst and many more had sought CO status. By the late 1990s, the number seeking CO status exceeded the number of draftees. In Russia in the 1990s, large numbers of young men sought to avoid conscription through bribery or educational attainment or medical excuse, while a small number of young men demonstrated the value of ACS as a civilian activity as opposed to noncombatant service in the military.

At the turn of the century, Germany appeared to be moving away from military conscription and toward greater opportunities for full-time volunteer service by young people. Although the number of COs continues to rise, the government reduced the budget for Zivildienst, thereby reducing the number of COs in Zivildienst and increasing the backlog of young men qualified as COs but not having served. The government also decided to recognize service of 12 months with Volunteer Social Year or Volunteer Ecology Year as completion of the service requirement, and was formulating plans to add a Volunteer Cultural Year and a Volunteer Sports Year to the full-time volunteer service options for young men and women.

> In Germany in 2001, I met both Zivildienst and Voluntary Social Year participants serving at a sheltered workshop for some 350 mentally retarded persons in Cologne. The cadets gave training and nurturing that enabled the persons to perform simple tasks such as inserting a machine part in a container and closing it with an identifying label. (DJE)

A continuing question in regard to alternative civilian service is how many of the large numbers of young men applying for CO status genuinely meet the definition of a CO as one who is conscientiously opposed to all wars. It is clear that many Americans took the CO position as selective COs with their opposition to the war in Vietnam. Similarly, many Russians would like to be COs because they do not want to fight in Chechneya, or simply because of the reputedly unsavory conditions of life as a draftee in the army.

> In Russia in 2001, I met a young man in Moscow who was one of about 90 Conscientious Objectors who were trying to convince the government that Alternative Service − a right guaranteed by the Constitution − should be performed under civilian auspices rather than military. He was working in Moscow with a group called Humanitarian Compassion and Charitable Center.

Because it is so difficult to distinguish between genuine COs and selective COs, or simply those who do not want to be soldiers for whatever reason, a number of countries have followed Germany's course and essentially permitted young men to choose their form of service, with civilian service of longer duration than military. In Italy, for example, the Parliament passed a law in 1972 that recognized conscientious objection to military service. The Ministry of Defense was instructed to organize and supervise the alternative service program for COs. They did so, although there was continuing tension between the Ministry of Defense and the CO community. With a term of service about 40 percent longer than military service, the number of COs rose gradually from a few hundred in the mid-1970s to a few thousand in the mid-1980s.

An Italian Court decision in 1989 equalized the terms of service and the numbers showed a marked increase, reaching about 80,000 in 1998. The Parliament decided in 2001 to discontinue military conscription in 2007 and to introduce a voluntary NYS that would co-exist with ACS until the end of the draft and continue afterward. The government subsequently decided to end the draft in 2005 and established a National Service Office, which administered both ACS and the voluntary NYS. (Palazzini, 2002)

As with Germany and Italy, at the turn of the century France was in the process of moving from a conscript military to a volunteer military, while at the same time transforming its ACS program to one of voluntary civil service. Under the new scheme, its NYS cadets are to receive a stipend of about half the minimum wage, but the stipend is to be tax-free and the cadets are to be eligible for an array of social security benefits, including maternity care, illness, and workplace accidents.

The ACS option has been available to young men in Hungary since 1989. It enrolls about 5,000 young men for a period of 15 months.

A variation on the ACS theme was introduced in the Philippines in 2002 with the cancellation of required military training for male university students and the introduction of a requirement that all university students choose between military training and community service.

Citizenship, Solidarity, and Nation-Building

Closely related to the trends away from military conscription and toward an expanded definition of volunteer service is the shift in the relationship of the citizen and the state. Until well into the 20th Century in much of the world, citizens were seen as subjects of the state. The role of the monarch or other head of state was to give orders and the role of the citizen was to obey them.

As citizens acquired rights, they also acquired responsibilities. They gained the right of suffrage, and elected the men and women who would govern their countries. Reciprocally, they gained the responsibility to participate in civil society. This responsibility underlay the rationale for young people to serve their communities and their nations, not as slaves or serfs but as citizens making the transition from adolescence to adulthood.

Nation-building as a rationale for NYS is found primarily in newly independent countries, many of whose borders were drawn by European colonial powers and bear little relationship to the ethnic divisions that had existed for centuries. The variety of NYS programs that have been created in the latter part of the 20th Century to promote nation-building illustrate the many components of nation-building, from the urban-rural divide to language barriers to age-old tribal divisions.

Indonesia's war of independence in the late 1940s led directly to the adoption of NYS. During the war, guerrillas who had some education taught school when they were not fighting. They saw the potential danger in the big difference in lifestyles between urban and rural areas. They wanted future leaders to be familiar with life in rural areas.

With independence in 1950, Indonesia established NYS for university graduates that provided teachers for secondary schools and teacher training colleges. By the mid-1960s, the educational system was producing enough teachers so the focus of NYS was changed to rural service projects. Kuliah Kerja Nyata (KKN), which means "learning through real work," was instituted in 1967 and places teams of one or two professors and about a dozen students to undertake village projects. The teams are multidisciplinary, utilize their education in their service activities, and reflect on the educational implications of their service experiences.

> In Indonesia in 1987 I visited Bantul, a small village near Yogyakarta, where KKN students from Gadjah Mada University were completing a water installation. They had tapped into a stream coming down a mountainside and built small reservoirs and a sedimentation tank, with pipes running to each house in the village. (DJE)

University coordinators work closely with the team and with village leaders to design projects that will be useful to the village and that can be accomplished by the KKN team. The projects are sometimes completed by a single team and at other times by a succession of KKN teams. Villagers contribute to the project as well, typically by providing free labor and housing. While participation in KKN is required of students, it is optional for teachers. Still, many are encouraged to serve knowing that they will receive points toward promotion within the university if they serve.

Although evaluation of the Indonesian study-service programs has been limited, it is clear that the students make a distinct contribution to village life and that they come to appreciate life in the village. A student who had recently completed service in KKN told one of us (DJE), "Before KKN I was proud [conceited], now I feel smaller [more humble]."

In Canada, the government started Katimavik in 1977 in large part because of the separatist movement in Quebec. Katimavik -- an Inuit word meaning meeting place -- comprises service teams of 12 young people, half-male and half-female, one-third French speaking and two-thirds English speaking, and from all parts of Canada. They undertake a set of three-month service projects, one in Eastern Canada, one in the West and one in Central Canada.

Not only do these young people work together during the day, they also kept house together. At any one time two members are on duty at the Katimavik house and they are responsible for cleaning house, shopping and cooking. They even have a Katimavik cookbook.

Katimavik was well-received by the Canadian public but was not well enough entrenched to survive the change in governments in the mid-1980s. With the return of the Liberal Party to power in 1993, Katimavik was revived and by 2002 was enrolling nearly 1,000 cadets per year.

Chile introduced a nation-building form of NYS for recent university graduates in 1995. Known as Servicio Pais, it is much smaller than Nigeria's NYSC because there is no penalty for not serving. Still, applicants for Servicio Pais always exceed the number of places available, which in 2002 reached about 300. NYS cadets serve primarily in rural communities in such fields as education, small business development, housing, fisheries, and economic and environmental development. There is every indication that the program is achieving its purpose of nation-building, as villagers get a sense that the central government cares for their welfare, and as cadets often decide to pursue their careers in the villages where they served.

In Chile in 2002, I met with two recent university graduates who were serving with Servicio Pais in the fishing village of Becalamu. One was an economist and the other an environmentalist. They were working with union members to strengthen the hand of the fishermen in the prices received for fish, and with local schools to teach children about marine life. (DJE)

Higher Education

The strongest and probably most irreversible trend has been the growing linkage between civic service and higher education.   At the time India was becoming independent in 1947, Mahatma Gandhi invoked the military image in a challenge to his countrymen.   He urged India to form "a service army to undertake a thirteenfold constructive program to bring literacy and healthcare and schools and agricultural cooperation and decency to every village in India." (Wofford, 1998) Numerous studies of NYS have been made; probably the most comprehensive is the one entitled *National Service for Defense, Development and National Integration of India* by M. L. Chibber. (Chibber, 1995).

While there have been a number of interesting local NYS initiatives in India, the most significant government program is the National Service Scheme.   The scheme began in 1969 and in 2004 involved two million college students doing 240 hours of social service over a two-year period.   Although participation is not a degree requirement, students who serve may receive a certificate of performance and a special reward if they are judged to have made an extraordinary contribution. There is also a National Cadet Corps that was started in 1948. It involves about one million school and college students and, while it is primarily concerned with character development and motivation, does include some community service activities.

Like the NYS program of Nigeria described in the previous chapter, Ghana also established its National Service Scheme for university graduates in 1973.   With about 70 percent of cadets serving as teachers, Ghana's NYS has become an essential part of the teaching force.   Similar programs on a more voluntary basis, are found in China, Vietnam, and several Latin American countries.

Since 1975, the University of Costa Rica has made several months of community service a graduation requirement for all students.   The purposes of Trabajo Comunal Universitario are to return the benefits of education to society, solve concrete problems, raise the consciousness of students, and bring the university closer to the community.   Professors serve along with the students, encourage them to take an interdisciplinary approach to problem-solving, and reflect on their service experiences.

> In Costa Rica in 2000, I met about a dozen university students and one of their professors in Trabajo Comunal Universitario who were serving in a nursing home in San Jose for about 200 old people. They assisted them with physical therapy and helped them maintain an herb garden but clearly their most appreciated service was simply socializing with the residents. (DJE)

The National Service Scheme of India, Trabajo Comunal Universitario of Costa Rica, and KKN of Indonesia are often referred to as service-learning programs (see Chapter 5), in which the accomplishment of a needed task is integrated with educational growth. A growing number of schools and universities around the world are instituting service-learning programs. They may be found in countries as diverse as Cuba and the United States, China and the United Kingdom, Russia and Argentina. Service-learning programs in secondary and tertiary education often serve as an introduction to full-time service with NYS. Given the good sense, the momentum and the low cost of service-learning, we think it likely that it will be widespread around the world by about 2025.

Employment

A number of countries have adopted NYS programs primarily to increase the employability of young people. The emphasis in these programs is on skill training augmented with some service activities usually related to national development priorities. Some of these programs also aim to instill a sense of patriotism in the cadets. The results have been mixed, as the training activities are sometimes out of line with job prospects, and as the cadets and others become disillusioned with the program if they cannot move directly into regular employment.

The Zambia National Service began in 1963 as a military force. Then, as the need for a large military lessened, it moved to agricultural training. By the turn of the century its emphasis had shifted to service for development, including activities such as land clearing and road building. These activities enabled young people to develop skills and move into jobs. (Mweene, 1998)

The Gambia National Youth Service Scheme is one of the more highly structured employment models. It was founded in 1996 and enrolls men and women from 17 to 25 years of age for a period of two years. A six-week para-military training course is followed by 22 months of skills training and community service. The service concludes with cadets re-assembled for a de-briefing and award of national service certificates to successful cadets.

Brazil has a NYS program similar to The Gambia's, although less rigorous. It is called Servicio Civil Voluntario and recruits 18-year-old young men and women living in poverty areas and with little formal education. Service projects include food distribution, health care programs, day care activities, and environmental activities. The enrollment period is six months which includes at least one month of community service together with work training, citizenship development, and basic education. While the program is run by the central government, it is operated by a number of NGOs. The program began in 1998 with a goal of eventually enrolling at least 50,000 young people. 14,000 cadets served with the program in 2000.

Employment is often a positive outcome of NYS programs not designed for that purpose. Large numbers of Peace Corps Volunteers have found jobs with the USA State Department. German members of Zivildienst and of Volunteer Social Year often find employment in the fields in which they served.

In Finland in 2001 I had lunch with a young man who had recently completed his Alternative Civilian Service where he had been assigned to work with members of minority groups, assisting them in areas such as employment and housing. Following completion of his service he was given a job with the government ministry dealing with minority groups. (DJE)

Service Delivery

Some of the most successful NYS programs were founded primarily as vehicles for the delivery of services to the needy or to the environment. They have the potential to develop into much larger programs.

Mexico's NYS began in 1936 with the assignment of medical students nearing completion of their studies to rural areas where there was no medical care. Some 1,000 students served for six months and submitted detailed reports including information about nutrition, sanitation, and types of illness. Not only did the reports have a powerful impact on the provision of public health services in rural areas, they also led to a 1947 law requiring all university students to serve for six months to two years. However, no federal funding was provided, as it had been for the medical students, so the execution was left up to the universities. As might be expected, the results were mixed. It is strongest in the medical field; in other areas the strength of Servicio Social varies with the university and the faculty.

In the United Kingdom, Community Service Volunteers was launched in 1961 as a private sector program challenging young people to give a year of service. It has since obtained partial governmental support and grown in size and scope.

In Wales in 1998, a young man in uniform arrived in a utility vehicle to pick me up and show me some conservation projects near Usk. He had just completed a year as a Community Service Volunteer where he had been assigned to the Conservation Service and where much of his work involved conducting ecological tours for school children in the area. He had just been hired as a full-time employee to continue the work and take on other responsibilities as well.

Like Nigeria's National Youth Service Corps, Ghana's National Service Scheme began in 1973 and assigns recent university graduates throughout the country for a year of service. Its primary aim is to compensate for manpower shortages in rural and other deprived areas of Ghana. Most are assigned as teachers and others as community workers, especially in the areas of public health and cooperative credit unions. The secondary aim is to promote national integration and cohesion by acquainting cadets with parts of Ghana they are not familiar with, thereby giving them a fuller understanding of their country and of the needs of poor areas.

President Bill Clinton started AmeriCorps in 1993 and it has since acquired the endorsement of President George W. Bush. AmeriCorps, whose motto is "Getting things done", enrolled some 50,000 young people in 2002 to serve full-time for nine months to a year in a wide variety of locally-organized community projects and in a number of conservation activities. AmeriCorps cadets receive financial assistance for education and training.

Under the umbrella of the Chinese Young Volunteers Association, China started the Poverty Alleviation Relay Project in 1994 to encourage university graduates to serve for a year or two in villages in central and western China. About 70 percent serve as teachers, the others in the fields of health and agriculture. Those who serve gain special recognition for future employment.

Vietnam launched a small NYS program in 1995 in an effort to have more university graduates work outside the big cities. Known as the "Organization of Young Intellectuals participating in Rural and Mountainous Development," 250 cadets served from 1995-97 primarily in the fields of public health, literacy, agriculture, and economic development. Sixty percent of them then stayed on as regular employees. In the 2000-2002 biennium, 500 cadets were serving in remote areas.

Volunteer Service

Second, just as military service was transformed in the 20th Century, so was the perception and nature of volunteer service. In many non-Western countries volunteer service was seen as an obligation of members of an extended family or of a community. Members served others when needed, and their service was reciprocated. In Western countries, volunteer service was seen as a kind of noblesse oblige, where the upper class people had an obligation to be generous to those in need. Volunteers were not paid, and governments were not involved with volunteer service

Times have changed. The sense of obligation has expanded beyond family members and rich people. The governments of Nigeria and Ghana decided in 1973 that university graduates had an obligation to give a year of service, usually in their fields of study. The official guidelines for the International Year of the Volunteer in 2001 said volunteer service "is for and about all kinds of volunteers everywhere; it is not limited to any one category of volunteer, whether formal or informal…domestic or international, unremunerated or modestly remunerated…." The guidelines also pointed to "volunteer service schemes as accepted alternatives …to military conscription."

In the 1960s the US government established the Peace Corps and paid stipends to volunteers in service. Corporations have adopted a stance of being socially responsible, and have permitted and sometimes encouraged their employees to spend some time in volunteer service. Yet it is interesting to note that the stipends given to Peace Corps Volunteers are often greater than the salaries paid to persons from the host country doing the same work, and many corporate employees still receive their executive salaries while doing volunteer service.

In the United States, the sense of obligation has extended to secondary schools. Since about 1990, the state of Maryland and a number of cities in America have made a period of community service a graduation requirement. These actions were challenged by civil libertarians on the grounds that they violated the constitutional restrictions on compulsory service. When the appeal reached the Supreme Court, they rejected it, essentially agreeing with the lower court decision that community service was as much a part of the educational process as the study of history or mathematics, which were also required for graduation.

Clearly then, volunteer service is widening its scope. It has extended to those in the Peace Corps and the United Nations Volunteers who receive stipends, to those in educational institutions whose service is seen to be a vital part of the educational process, and to those in countries where service is seen to be a responsibility of citizenship. And the sponsorship of volunteer service has broadened beyond families and neighborhoods and non-governmental organizations (NGOs) to governments and intergovernmental agencies.

International Service

The twin goals of most international youth service programs are the delivery of needed services and improved understanding among people of different countries. These programs began with the launching of Service Civile Internationale and the voluntary workcamp movement. As the international secretary of the Fellowship of Reconciliation, Pierre Ceresole of Switzerland was the prime mover in the establishment of what is generally recognized as the first international voluntary workcamp in 1920, near Verdun, site of one million deaths in a year-long battle in 1916. Ceresole, the son of a Swiss President, had strong Christian beliefs that led him to prison in both World Wars for refusal to pay war taxes. Since 1920, there have been numerous workcamps that have brought together young people from many countries to assist in reconstruction and rehabilitation following wars and natural disasters.

The organizations multiplied following World War II and may be found in Europe under names such as Associazione per la Formazione gli Scambi e le Attiva International,

Aktionsgemeinschaft Dienst fur den Frieden, Compagnons Batisseurs, and the European Federation for Intercultural Learning.

The United Nations has also played a role in international service. It established the Coordinating Committee for International Voluntary service in 1948 and continues to support it through UNESCO. The United Nations Volunteers (UNV) is a global service program but since its founding in 1971 most of its participants have been mid-level career people aged 30 to 50. UNV did make an opening to younger participants in 2000 with the decision to accept an Italian offer to place recent university graduates as UNV interns for one year of service outside of Italy.

Beginning with the UK's Voluntary Service Overseas (VSO) in 1959, several countries have initiated unilateral programs of overseas service, primarily for young adults. VSO was followed in the early 1960s by America's Peace Corps, Canada's Canadian University Service Overseas, and Japan's Overseas Cooperation Volunteers. France and Germany supported similar programs as alternatives to military service.

All of these international programs are small compared with the size of armies or even with the NYS programs in Germany and Nigeria. Still, the experience they have gained and the networks they have developed can be of great assistance in the expansion of international youth service programs.

The creation of the International Association for National Youth Service (IANYS) is another example of the global trend toward NYS. Founded at a global conference on NYS in Papua New Guinea in 1996 following previous global conferences in the United States and Nigeria, subsequent biennial meetings of IANYS have been held in the United Kingdom, Israel, Argentina, and Ghana.

Another example is the $3 million grant given by the Ford Foundation to the Center for Social Development at Washington University in St. Louis, USA in 2001 to create a Global Service Institute to conduct research on NYS globally, and to work on NYS policy and programs around the world.

The International Youth Parliament has a stronger service orientation than its name implies. It was founded by Oxfam in 2000 as a global network of young activists intent on building a peaceful, sustainable, and equitable world. The Youth Parliament convenes several hundred young activists every few years to network with one another, to make policy recommendations, and to return home to implement actions for social change.

Regional Trends

In Europe the principal trend toward NYS stems from the shift from military conscription to volunteer armies combined with the smaller size of armies and the inclusion of women in military service. Furthermore, the impressive example of Germany's Zivildienst has built confidence in other European countries that NYS can succeed on a sizable scale. An indication of the growing importance of NYS was the first conference on NYS convened by the European Union in 2003. Also, the most significant regional NYS is found in Europe with its European Voluntary Service, founded in 1996. It facilitates the placement of young people in NYS programs in other countries in the European Union, and has developed a clear allocation of responsibilities for the sending and receiving organizations as well as for the cadets.

In Latin America the major trend toward NYS is found in the joining of education with service. It is seen in service-learning programs, most notably in Argentina; in university programs where periods of service are integrated with university studies, most notably in Costa Rica; and in Chile's Servicio Pais where university graduates serve in rural communities.

In Africa, there appears to be a trend away from mandatory NYS programs and toward those that are more voluntary. In 2002, an official Nigerian government commission recommended a voluntary service as one of four options that might be introduced as a replacement for the existing National

Youth Service Crops.   Ghana initiated a voluntary NYS scheme in 2003 as a supplement to the existing mandatory scheme for university graduates.   Another African trend has been the gradual shift of several NYS programs from a strong military and skills training emphasis to a stronger service orientation.

The situation is more complex in Eastern Europe and Asia.   In Russia and a number of former Soviet-bloc states, one finds an abhorrence of state-run NYS programs as they are reminiscent of the state-controlled youth programs of Soviet times.   By contrast, in China, where the devolution of state control has been more gradual than it was in Russia, there appears to be general acceptance of state-run programs that are fairly decentralized and engage the talents and interests of the cadets.   India has its National Service Scheme, a National Cadet Corps and a large number of NGO youth initiatives.   A small but promising non-governmental Pakistan National Youth Service was started in 2003, and Japan's government sponsors domestic and overseas NYS programs, both on a fairly small scale.

Studies

A number of countries were studying or planning for NYS near the turn of the century.   Papua New Guinea's National Youth Service Commission developed a comprehensive plan for NYS on 1991.   Its National Service Scheme would have young people give two years of service either in the military or in civilian activities in fields such as education and health, and it would have university students give one year of service in rural villages, working in their fields of study.   Its Volunteer Service Scheme would encourage young people to volunteer to serve in their own communities, and a small number to serve overseas.   Fourteen years later, it had not received operational funding.

South Africa developed a somewhat similar plan for NYS in 1998.   Its National Youth Commission published a

Green Paper in setting forth a comprehensive NYS plan. Despite strong support from Nelson Mandela and many others, it has not yet been implemented because of cost considerations. However, a number of small projects are underway that could form the foundation of a future NYS.

One of us (Gal) developed a proposal in 1995 for a Civic Youth Service in Israel that would engage substantial numbers of young Jews and Arabs serving together on public service projects. The proposal appeared to be gaining support -- especially among young the youth population -- until 2000, when renewed hostilities between Israel and Palestine forced it to be put on hold.

Henning Sorenson of Denmark's Institute for Sociological Research made a study of NYS at the request of the government. His report was issued in 2001 and recommends a Civil Samfundspligt (NYS) of 40,000 young people serving for a period of seven months and receiving stipends equal to those of military conscripts. As of 2004, the government had not yet acted on the report.

*   *   *   *   *

While William James and Eugen Rosenstock-Huessy perceived NYS in its relationship to military service, that perception is gradually disappearing and is being replaced by a growing recognition of NYS as a policy that deserves serious consideration in areas such as education, employment, nation-building, and the provision of services to those in need. As everyone was reminded by the war in Iraq in 2003, world events can stop and even reverse these trends. In our view, however, they will do no more than delay the trend toward NYS in the short-term and may actually accelerate that trend as people and governments perceive the near futility of war and the potential of NYS.

CHAPTER 4

BEST PRACTICES OF NATIONAL YOUTH SERVICE

The basic features of NYS bear a striking resemblance to those of military service. They include provisions for recruitment, training, placement, and financial support. And they include issues, such as making the service voluntary or compulsory, deciding on the duration of service, and providing for post-service opportunities. This chapter examines these features and suggests the consequences of different choices. But first we must ask the question, as it is often asked about the military, what is the purpose of NYS?

For military service, the commonly accepted purpose is national defense, although history abounds with examples of more aggressive ambitions. Armies are also used for the maintenance of domestic law and order and in the performance of non-military service projects.

There was no commonly accepted purpose of NYS at the turn of the 21st Century. The NYS programs of the previous century had varied purposes, from conservation and income transfer in America's Civilian Conservation Corps, to reduction of draft inequities in Germany's Zivildienst, nation-building in Nigeria's National Youth Service Corps, and experiential education in Costa Rica's Trabajo Comunal Universitario.

The public perception of NYS also shows considerable variation. Some educators view it as a form of experiential education that complements classroom learning; others see it as reducing the time available to teachers to impart their knowledge in the classroom. Some employers view NYS as helpful in producing labor force entrants with solid work experience; others see it as introducing unfair competition into the marketplace. Some conservationists view NYS as a source of labor to help reduce air, water, and noise pollution, and to create healthier woodland and wilderness areas.

Some political scientists see NYS as a form of the social contract, in which NYS realizes the mutual responsibility that should exist between young people and society: on the part of the youth to serve the society which has nurtured and educated them, and on the part of society to give young people a wide range of opportunities to gain constructive experience in the world which will soon be theirs. Other political scientists view NYS as easing the way for governments to indoctrinate the young. Some sociologists see NYS as a structural system fostering social capital, while psychologists may emphasize NYS as a rite of passage from adolescence to adulthood, offering the kinds of personal challenges and opportunities that foster maturation and growth of self-confidence.

Some civil libertarians see NYS negatively, as a violation of personal freedom; others see it as positively, as a way to acquaint them with societal needs and to expose young people to people from different backgrounds. Economists' views of NYS range widely. Conservative economists may see NYS as a waste of money in a market economy on the theory that the interplay of the market determines which products and services are important. Liberal economists may see NYS as useless in a socialist economy where they believe any real needs should be met through governmental job creation. Some economists may see NYS as an "opportunity cost," where young people are denied the income they would receive in the marketplace; others they may see it as a boon to the economy because it increases the flow of money through the economy.

With this array of perceptions, it is little wonder that NYS does not easily come into focus. The public and politicians alike find it easier to understand programs along one dimension: if there is a health problem, send in the doctors; if adolescents need to know about career possibilities, add it to the school curriculum.

But as NYS programs with different purposes were implemented, it became clear that the multi-purpose nature of NYS was its greatest strength. The Zivildienst in Germany was supposed to equalize the hardships for soldiers and Conscientious Objectors (COs). In doing so, it resulted in a much needed-and much-appreciated delivery of services, combined with valuable work experience and career exploration for the COs. America's CCC, in addition to meeting the stated purposes of income transfer and conservation work, helped to transform millions of young men from a potential life of poverty and despair and alienation to patriotic and productive citizens and, eventually, to pillars of society.

Perhaps sometime in the future, the multipurpose nature of NYS will gain general recognition as a major part of a country's youth policy. In the more immediate future, we expect NYS programs will continue to be created for a variety of specified purposes, just as they were in the 20th Century. Whatever primary purpose a country may assign to NYS, certain features will be essential and a number of other features will have to be considered. The following section delineates the essential features of NYS, taking into consideration the viewpoints of the cadets who serve, the persons they serve, the organizations with which the cadets work, as well as the wider community and the nation.

Essential Features

The work done by cadets is important and is seen to be important by the cadets. In recent years the rationale for NYS in some countries has focused more on its value as a youth development program than on the importance of the services provided by cadets. As the last two chapters illustrate, there is good reason for this. But having this focus for NYS presents a problem. Unless well-designed and carefully monitored, there seems to be a tendency to want to do more and more things to the youthful participants, with the inevitable consequence that there is less time for them to serve others. In Canada's Katimavik, for example, with cadets serving in three different localities, spending one out of six weeks keeping house, and another few weeks in language practice, the impact of their service activities is inevitably diluted. Bill Clinton seemed to be aware of this by making the motto of AmeriCorps, "Getting things done."

Here again, there is a parallel with military service. Nations do not create armies for the purpose of youth development; they create them for the purpose of national defense and occasionally for conquest. Still, they are de facto youth development programs, as millions of veterans would be prepared to testify.

The common element among the largest and most successful NYS programs is the delivery of needed services. Conservation work was a major aim of America's CCC, and for the next half century its members could be seen in the nation's parks and forests proudly showing their children and grandchildren the cabins they built and the trails they blazed.

The most widely acclaimed accomplishment of Fidel Castro's Cuba was the near-elimination of illiteracy in 1961, largely through the efforts of the 100,000 young people who went to the countryside and taught people how to read and write. Although the literacy campaign was a short-term effort, the linkage between school and community has continued:

In Cuba in 1977, I visited a kindergarten where students were weeding the lettuce and radish plants they had planted a few weeks earlier, an elementary school where the children were packaging tea into small bags for sale, a high school where students were making baseballs, a dairy farm which doubled as a residential high school where students took regular high school classes and learned farming by doing chores, and a university where medical students were serving in a clinic. (DJE)

The work done by Germany's Zivildienst had become so important by the 1990s that Germany postponed a move from military conscription to an All-Volunteer Force. The educational, agricultural, and community development sectors of Nigeria were substantially advanced in the last quarter of the 20th Century by the hundreds of thousands of university graduates who served in the NYSC.

When a youth service program fails to do important work, it becomes very bad policy indeed. In the USA in the 1960s, Congress feared urban uprisings in the summer and in May passed legislation creating summer work programs for about one million young people, beginning in June. Many of the cities receiving the money were not able to organize that much work in such a short time. The result was that when the young people turned up on Monday to be assigned to summer jobs, they were told to go away and return on Fridays to get paid. Getting paid for work that is not done teaches the wrong lesson and gives no help to the people who might have been served.

That kind of situation also leads to suggestions that there is too little important work to engage all young people for a year of service. Yet in the USA in the late 1990s, with unemployment hovering below what used to be called the frictional level of four percent, some 40,000 AmeriCorps members were usefully engaged in service activities in a way that was supported by Republican and Democratic politicians alike. And in the welfare state of Germany in the 1980s and 90s, an average of 100,000 young men in Zivildienst could be found at any one time performing services that had not previously been met. Where surveys have been done, the service needs of society have been shown to exceed the size of a single year youth cohort. And most charitable agencies say they need many more employees and volunteers to help with their work.

We disagree with the idea that the interest of labor or business should take absolute priority over the interest of service. Regardless of the form of government, humanitarian and environmental needs exist in every country in the world. Should they be left to fester just because trade union leaders think that paying market wages is more important than meeting human and environmental needs, or because business leaders have the idea that the economic marketplace solves all problems of supply and demand?

It is worth noting that many NGOs would hire more people if they had the money. Utilizing NYS cadets enables them to expand and improve their delivery of services. Also, NYS can be a job creator, as it is with NGOs that engage a cadet -- perhaps because they think it is a nice thing to do – and discover after a year of service that the work the cadet was doing was important enough to justify hiring someone for the job.

Recruitment of cadets is tailored to the extent service is a requirement. If military service is part of a young person's obligation upon reaching 18, he or she goes to a post office or recruitment center to sign up and awaits his or her call-up notice. Similarly, if voluntary service is very attractive, the government need do little more than put out an official notice of where to sign up and young people will flock to enroll.

When NYS is a well-established requirement, young people generally accept the obligation to serve as readily as they accept other requirements.   Thus, Nigerian secondary school students going on to university understand that a year of service following graduation is as much a part of getting a professional job as is the university degree. And teenagers in a number of American cities and states understand that a period of community service during high school is as much a graduation requirement as is the study of English and history.

When the service is not some kind of requirement and quotas are not met through minimal effort, then the government must advertise. The kind of advertising that is done helps to determine the kinds of young people who volunteer their services. Mayor Ed Koch of New York City established the City Volunteer Corps in the early 1980s and feared that a volunteer program would attract primarily white college graduates, as had happened with the Peace Corps. Accordingly, he targeted the recruitment campaign at black and disadvantaged young people with the result that hardly anyone outside the target group volunteered for service. When later they tried to change the image, to make it more appealing across the board, it took several years to shake the image that had been created through the early campaign.

A rigorous test of NYS was conducted in Seattle in 1973-74. It was well-researched, and has yielded some of the most reliable data on NYS. The experiment was conducted in the mid-1970s by America's federal volunteer agency known as ACTION in the city of Seattle and the surrounding area. The government wanted to see how many young people would come forward if all had the opportunity to do so, how many and what kinds of service positions could be made available in the community, what the socioeconomic profile of cadets would be, the value of services rendered, and the impact of the experience on the cadets. The service period was one year and all the cadets came from, and served in, the Seattle area. A three-stage recruitment effort had been planned with the understanding that it would be stopped if and when the budget limitations were reached. However, that happened during the first stage.

A survey determined that 25 percent of the eligible population of 80,000 were aware of the service program. Of those who were aware, 10 percent of the young men and women eligible for the program sent in applications. All were invited to a one-day orientation session and half of them actually appeared. At the same time government agencies and NGOs in the area were invited to request NYS cadets and 221 did so, listing some 1,200 available positions. The young people reviewed the available positions, went for interviews with those that interested them, and signed an agreement if both parties agreed to it. Over the course of two months, 372 young people – about two percent of those who were aware of the opportunity to serve -- entered service. Sponsors put up five percent of the stipend. (Kappa Systems, Inc. 1975)

The socio-economic profile of cadets was fairly close to that of young people in the test area, although young women, unemployed persons, and the better-educated persons were somewhat over-represented.

Under certain circumstances, a conflict between NYS and military recruitment may arise and the question will be asked, "Will national security be threatened when military quotas are not met because of the number of young people entering NYS?" Not necessarily. The problem can be solved by the order of call into military service. Everyone would be registered for service at, say, age 18, and could opt for military or civilian service before the age of, say, 24, or make no choice. The first to be taken into military service would be those who had opted for it upon registration, then those who had not opted for any service, then those who had opted for civilian service but not yet entered it, then those in civilian service, and lastly those who had completed a military or civilian service period. Thus, the size of the pool of potential military personnel would remain unchanged. Another approach to the problem would be to limit enrollment in NYS to those persons who are either not required by the military or who qualify as Conscientious Objectors.

The central government challenges young people to serve. During World War II, the most common poster in American cities and villages was of Uncle Sam pointing his finger and saying, "I want you." What he wanted everyone for was to make bombs and bullets on the home front or go overseas and put one's life on the line to defeat the enemy. NYS need not be bashful in stating why it needs young people. It should communicate this message: "There is a lot of work to be done that is not being done. There are trees to be planted, trails to be built, children to be cared for, immigrants to be taught to read and write our language, old people living at home to be given a little help to enable them to stay at home and not go to a nursing home. We ask you to invest in your fellow man and your country for a year."

Support for NYS comes from those who benefit from it. Although military service generally derives 100 percent of its support from the central government, that is not required for NYS. When NYS programs are analyzed, we see that benefits accrue to the persons served, to the cadets who serve, to the community where they serve, to their future employers, and to the nation as a whole. Appropriate levels of support should come from the beneficiaries.

As the poor and disabled are usually unable to pay for the services they receive, the organization through which cadets serve can contribute on their behalf.   Thus, if NYS cadets serve the mentally ill, it could come from a mental health association or the Ministry of Health. If a substantial share of that contribution comes from the organization where the young person is serving, it helps to insure that the cadets will be assigned to important jobs.

In return for the benefits of work experience, career exploration, and others, NYS cadets contribute by receiving a stipend below market level.

Future employers benefit by getting former cadets as employees with work experience, with a sense of what they want to work on, and sometimes by identifying future employees through NYS.

Benefits to the community and nation are quite varied, including lower payouts for the unemployed, and accomplishing more and better service at lower cost. The local contribution is often in the provision of food and housing. The nation often contributes a major part of the stipend together with providing recruitment, orientation, and other support services.

In fact, NYS is often strengthened when support comes from more than one source, especially in situations where cadets are serving with local governments or NGOs.

NYS cadets and host organizations receive appropriate orientation and training. Cadets undergo a period of orientation so they will understand procedures regarding medical care, vacation time, payment of stipends, living and travel arrangements. This can be done in about three days.

Host organizations also require training as to the unique nature of NYS cadets. The omission of this requirement in the experimental NYS program in Seattle proved to be its weakest link. Some sponsors took advantage of the optional half-day orientation that was offered. However, many did not, and it was among this group that a disproportionately high number of failures was found.

The only essential training in NYS is that geared to the work to be done. Thus, training is most often conducted by the host organization and can be done in a few days or perhaps a week or two. Often it is a matter of a cadet's supervisor giving special attention to the cadet during her first few weeks in service. Where a team of cadets is serving in one place, the training occurs in a group and is somewhat more formal.

Some NYS programs offer training which may not be essential to cadet assignments but which is considered highly beneficial. Thus, literacy classes are given to those who cannot read or write. Training in first aid, personal hygiene, and computer skills may be given to all cadets. Skills training may be given as well, especially to cadets with little education.

Cadets have a decision-making role in NYS. Young people in a country with a volunteer military can choose whether or not to serve and, if they decide to serve, what branch of service they will enter. In a conscript military, many young men "volunteer" for the Navy or some other branch of service viewed as less arduous or more challenging than the one they would have been drafted into had they waited. Of course, once a person enters the military, certain things are compulsory.

Similarly, young people should have certain choices concerning NYS. It is especially appropriate in selecting the kind of service to perform and the time and place – within given options -- where they will do it. These choices can apply even in programs with a high degree of compulsion. In

Germany's Zivildienst, for example, some 90 percent of those who enter choose from a large menu of approved organizations where they will interview and once accepted, the Zivildienst authority approves the position. In addition to guaranteeing higher motivation, this enables the cadets to build the NYS period into their career plans, just as they do with higher education or overseas travel. Similarly, they are able to test out career options in NYS.

Cadets serve in teams, even when placements are individual. Teams are at the heart of military organization. The basic unit is the squad or platoon and several of them comprise a company and so on. NYS cadets can serve in teams or as individuals. NYS activities such as conservation work and emergency relief require teams which, like squads in the army, comprise about a dozen persons. They train together, serve together and, in residential programs, may also live together.

Alternatively, individual placements are appropriate for activities such as teaching and home health aides. But even there it may be useful to form teams of 10 or 12 serving in the same neighborhood. Teams are a way to promote understanding among cadets from different parts of the country, different races, different income levels, and different religious and cultural backgrounds.

These forms of integration are a high priority in Canada's Katimavik. Twelve-person teams are composed of a representative sample of Canada's youth population, with half male and half female, four from French-speaking Quebec and eight from assorted English-speaking provinces. These teams, together with an adult supervisor live together in Katimavik houses. They do the housework and take turns grocery shopping and cooking, a task taken so seriously that two of the cadets are released from their service assignments for two week periods to do these tasks.

Similar team mixes can be found in programs such as City Year, which originated in Boston in 1988 and came under the AmeriCorps umbrella shortly after its establishment in 1993.

City Year, which by 2000 had expanded to several other cities, has many individual placements but makes up teams which are deliberately integrated, comprising young people of different races, sexes, educational backgrounds, and social classes. The teams meet frequently as a group to discuss their activities and deal with problems that arise. Every workday begins with all the teams assembling in the city plaza for announcements, exercise, esprit de corps, and public relations.

Nigeria's NYSC uses individual placements but achieves a measure of integration first by assigning cadets to serve in parts of the country far removed from their home towns, and second by arranging weekly meetings of cadets serving in the same area. There they discuss their activities, deal with administrative matters, and plan a project that they will do as a team. Israel's NYS also makes up teams among cadets placed individually.

A country or region that wants NYS to strengthen linkages among a diverse population will find that NYS teams help to integrate society and add to its social capital.

The duration of service is 9 months to two years. The first month consists of orientation and training and getting acquainted with the place of assignment and the work to be done. During this time the productivity of the cadet is virtually zero. The next two months the cadet is in service and is on a sharp learning curve as he or she learns what to do and what not to do. The cadet starts being productive during this period but the costs of supervision and lost time and mistakes often exceed the cost of services rendered. By the fourth month the cadet starts becoming a net producer and by the sixth month his total productivity has about equaled what has been spent on him. Thus, a service period of nine months pretty much assures that the value of the services given by the cadet will exceed his cost. As overseas service is more expensive than domestic service, we suggest a minimum service period of one year.

Two years is sufficient time for NYS cadets to render services valued at greater cost than that of the cadets, and to reap the several benefits of serving in NYS, yet not too long as likely to cause burnout. Those who want to remain with NYS in some way might take supervisory positions in the field or other administrative positions in NYS. Thus, the optimal duration of a cadet's national service is between nine months and two years. Shorter periods fail to yield the above benefits and longer periods become exploitative of the cadets and risk burnout.

If national service is to attract a substantial proportion of young people, it must offer a strong incentive for service. Thus, large numbers of Americans joined the CCC because doing so provided some relief from the extreme poverty faced by their families. The Nigerian Youth Service Corps has a very high participation rate because refusal means they are not eligible for employment in Nigeria. In Germany, some young men are genuine COs while others in Zivildienst find a period of civilian service to be a more agreeable option than a somewhat shorter period of military service. By contrast NYS programs which offer little external incentive but rely on the young person's inherent incentive to serve, have much smaller enrollments, as with Volunteer Social Year in Germany and Servicio Pais in Chile.

Opportunities for reflection on the service experience are an integral part of NYS. Cadets will learn a lot anyway but will learn more if they are encouraged to reflect on their experiences and if there is some structure for doing so. There are a variety of ways their learning can be enhanced.

Once they have their assignments but before beginning their service, cadets can develop a learning framework for their experiences. They can describe what they think the experience will be like and later compare it with the reality. They can make a list of questions about the work they will do and see how many are answered. They can describe elements of their character and outlook that they think will be changed by the experience. They can borrow from the fields of sociology and psychology to posit behaviors they think they will observe.

Cadets can keep daily diaries of their activities and observations. Educational institutions can recognize the learning acquired by cadets during their service. Self-reflection and information exchange can be done through means such as periodic seminars and evaluation of academic papers written by cadets. In NYS programs which are faith-based or have a strong religious component, certain types of religious seminars may be integrated into the service period. Such is the case, for example, in two of the "Sherut Leumi" programs in Israel which are open, specifically, for young women from orthodox Jewish families only.

Cadets receive appropriate recognition and benefits. Cadets should receive a certificate of completion that gives their dates in service, where they served, and a brief description of their service activities. Cadets may also be invited to prepare a statement on their service, giving such things as the skills acquired and the learning derived from the service activities. Where cadets' service and learning are well integrated, as they are in Costa Rican and Indonesian universities, and in many elementary and secondary schools in Argentina and the USA, academic credit may be awarded on the basis of the learning acquired.

Nigeria's NYSC conducts what is probably the most comprehensive recognition of service. As their service year approaches its end, cadets return to camp near the state capitol where they discuss their experiences and make recommendations for improvement. Then they proceed to the capitol where they march in a passing-out parade and receive their certificates of national service, with honors for outstanding service awarded to selected cadets. In Israel, upon completion of service, Sherut Leumi graduates are entitled to the same benefits and privileges awarded to military veterans.

However, governments and NGOs have to be careful not to overload the benefits of NYS because doing so will motivate young people to enroll largely for selfish reasons and the necessary dedication to serving those in need will be eroded.

Positive opportunities are available after service in NYS. Those cadets who have completed NYS successfully should be entitled to favorable opportunities for further education and for employment. The NYS experience is a main avenue to such opportunities, as cadets develop career plans, acquire work experience, and expand their network of acquaintances. The NYS administration can help by arranging meetings for cadets prior to their departure where they may be instructed in techniques of job-seeking, and informed of avenues to further education and training.

NYS develops gradually, giving priority to quality over quantity. Rapid NYS mobilizations have been successful, as when America's CCC enrollment went from zero to 250,000 over the course of three months in 1933. However, the US Army mobilized the CCC, and it was carried out in the context of a great national cause.

Looked at from the standard of efficiency, most NYS programs would benefit from a gradual introduction. It is good to begin with pilot projects to test out various approaches and to refine the process. Are the host agencies performing well? Are the team leaders performing well? Do they need more training? Is NYS attracting volunteers from across the socio-economic spectrum? The gradual build-up can be accomplished over the course of a few years and the program can then be expanded with confidence.

Optional Elements

Should all young people be entitled to serve in NYS? We believe they should be. The universality of military service varies with the need and the circumstances. At university in 1947 one of us (Eberly) was rejected by the mandatory Reserve Officers Training Corps for failure to pass the eye examination. Four years later, at the height of American involvement in the Korean War, he was called up for military service and although his eyesight had worsened, passed the eye exam and was inducted into the Army.

The Israeli Defense Force has no Arabs. Conscription is more widely applied to men than to women. US forces were not integrated until about 1947 but once they were, the opportunities for blacks expanded more rapidly than in any other sector of society.

Limiting the universality of NYS limits the extent to which NYS can meet its promise. If NYS accepts only the well-educated, it will widen the gulf between them and the poorly educated as the latter will miss out on the benefits of the NYS experience. If NYS takes only the poorly educated, both cadets and the public will view it as a program that further stigmatizes the poorly educated. If NYS is limited in size, it will exclude some who will miss out on its benefits.

The initial purpose of NYS often dictates the degree to which it is universal. Thus, Germany's Zivildienst is limited to men (as is the case in the Bundeswehr), while Nigeria's NYSC enrolls only graduates of tertiary institutions, as part of its "melting pot" mission. Likewise, Israel's NYS started with primarily Jewish women and had no Arab citizens -- as is the case in the military. Both of these restrictions were lifted at the beginning of the century.

We suggest that NYS be open to all young people with very few exceptions. In 1966, when the rejection rate of young Americans called for military service was 33 percent, it was estimated it would be about 10 percent for NYS candidates. Persons who were severely physically and mentally impaired would be excluded, while persons who were blind or deaf or mildly retarded would be accepted. Such a standard requires a wide enough array of service opportunities to insure that all those willing to serve can find a position.

A universal service need not be compulsory. Like voting in national elections, NYS can be open to everyone but without penalty for not participating. Participation rates will increase as NYS is made more attractive to young people, whether through material benefits such as level of stipend and entitlement to further education, or non-material benefits such as offering young people adventurous assignments or the chance to test out possible careers of interest to them.

Should NYS be voluntary or compulsory? In the ideal society, service should be entirely voluntary, just as school attendance and payment of taxes and obeying the law should be voluntary. In the real world, nations have found it necessary to introduce a measure of compulsion in order to accomplish those things a society considers important. They institute penalties for the infringement of such requirements. The penalties vary greatly according to the magnitude of the offense, from a child being kept after school to a rich person fined for tax avoidance to a murderer being executed.

We suggest that the appropriate degree of compulsion for NYS in most countries is about in the middle of the continuum between total compulsion and total voluntariness. We do not suggest penalties for those refusing service in NYS, rather rewards for those who serve. Thus, there would be no jail sentences or fines for those who do not serve. Rather, those who serve would gain entitlement to one or more benefits in areas such as education, employment, and housing. Such systems are already in place and are working well in Israel, China, and the United States.

Furthermore, the distinction between voluntary and compulsory service is a false dichotomy, for two reasons. First, no NYS is totally voluntary or totally compulsory. In voluntary programs, cadets must meet certain standards relating to behavior and showing up to work on time, while in compulsory programs cadets have choices, such as emigrating from Germany to avoid military service or Zivildienst, or not entering university in Nigeria.

Second, the individual perception of what is voluntary and what is compulsory shows great variation. A wealthy young person who can choose among further education and world travel and employment in the family firm may oppose compulsory service, as it restricts his options. By contrast, an inner-city school dropout from a poor family may have only two choices, namely, crime and extreme poverty. Compulsory NYS increases his choices and offers a way out of the situation.

Voluntarism vs. compulsion is at once the most controversial and the most confusing issue of NYS and can usefully be examined from several perspectives, beginning with the military experience.

•During the 20th century, nations instituted compulsory military service when they considered it to be in the national interest. Especially in times of emergency, almost everyone who was drafted went willingly and some young men chose to volunteer for military service. There was little if any distinction between those who entered, whether voluntarily or compulsorily, nor was there any noticeable difference in the performance of volunteers and draftees. The public-at-large viewed military service as a responsibility of citizenship.

•By contrast, NYS was only rarely seen as a responsibility of citizenship. It was in 1961 when large numbers of young Cubans were mobilized to teach illiterates to read and write, and did so with great success. It was the case with the barefoot doctors of China who, though with rudimentary training, contributed to the health of those they served where well-trained doctors were not available. It was the case among the majority Jewish population of Israel, where there was virtually total support for young people in service, almost all of whom were engaged in military or civilian service. The concept of NYS as a citizenship responsibility continued throughout the century: in China and Cuba as service was fostered as a part of the continuing revolution, and as Israel remained under military threat.

•Compulsory community service is increasingly being recognized as a citizenship responsibility in the United States. In the 1980s, a number of schools made service-learning a graduation requirement. Then the movement spread to cities like Atlanta and states like Maryland. Before long, some parents objected to schools imposing compulsory service on the grounds that it was involuntary servitude, forbidden by the Constitution. The case made by supporters of the service requirement was that the service was a form of experiential education and as such, an important part of the educational process, similar to the inclusion of laboratory periods in the teaching of physics and chemistry. Eventually the Supreme Court upheld a lower court ruling that if a school system decided that service was important to a student's education, it could be required. As evidence of the widening definition of volunteerism, many schools with a service-learning requirement continue to refer to it as volunteer service and to the students as volunteers.

•In Ethiopia in the early 1960s, Emperor Haile Selassie created the Ethiopian University Service that required university students to spend a year teaching in village schools around the country. A pre-service survey found that many students were skeptical about the value of the year of mandatory service, but in the post-service survey the students gave overwhelming support to the program. When asked whether it should be voluntary or compulsory, some 90 percent said it should be remain compulsory for the reason that students would not know how valuable the experience would be and few would volunteer for it. (Korten, 1969)

20th Century societies that viewed NYS as important introduced various penalties and rewards to foster participation. Unemployed young men in America in the 1930s were not required to join the CCC but millions were motivated to do so by the attraction of three square meals a day and money for their families to buy food and clothing.   Young Nigerians knew that they would have to serve in the NYSC for a year if they completed their university studies.   Young German men could essentially choose between a period of required military service or a one-third longer period of civilian service.   University graduates in China knew that teaching for a year or two in a village Western China would virtually guarantee them a good job and good housing on completion of service.

Probably the biggest challenge for compulsory NYS programs is maintaining the public's view of them as reasonable.   There are many ways they can go wrong.   As Nigeria went through military coups and governmental corruption, university students and others began to question the legitimacy of a program requiring them to serve at low pay while those who imposed the requirement were living off the fat of the land.   In the US state of Maryland that established 75 hours of community service as graduation requirement from secondary school, a number of schools decided to do it on the cheap and instead of hiring a service-learning coordinator, told the students to arrange their own service experiences.   This led many students to invent various ways to get around the requirement and created a general disdain for it.

An argument sometimes put forward in opposition to compulsory programs is that they result in a poor quality of service.   Our observations suggest that is not the case when cadets understand and accept the rationale for the compulsion, and when the program is well administered.   Thus, Nigerian cadets who are teaching school perform at the same level as the salaried employees teaching in the same school.   The German members of Zivildienst doing the same jobs as members of the Voluntary Social Year perform them just as well.

There is no question but what compulsory programs can be worse than no program at all.   However, we are convinced that NYS programs with some degree of compulsion are not automatically bad things.   Having positive outcomes to

NYS, in respect to those who are served, to the cadets who serve, to the community and to the nation, has more to do with five other factors.

First, the reason for the compulsion must be acceptable to those who serve. Following the revolutions in China and Cuba, young people accepted that their service was important in building a new state. They talked of continuing the revolution, but with civilian means rather than military. In Germany following the re-introduction of military conscription in 1956, young men understood that where military service was required of some, reasons of equity dictated that some form of service be required of all.

Second, the program must deliver valued services. Thus, a central body could approve organizations to host cadets and those organizations could determine the tasks they want the cadets to undertake.

Third, the service activities must utilize the talents and interests of the cadets. Thus, the university graduates in Nigeria's NYSC and China's PARP are assigned as teachers, medical personnel, and other professional roles consistent with their levels of education.

Fourth, compulsory NYS programs fare better when cadets are given options. Cadets should have a say as to where and when they serve. They should have a range of choices of their assignments, although there are notable exceptions. One of the biggest problems found in a review of Nigeria's National Youth Service Corps in 2002 was the pressure put on officials of the NYSC by cadets and members of their extended families to assign cadets to locations of their choice. (Federal Ministry, 2002) Admittedly, giving them some degree of choice over service location would to some extent vitiate the scheme's goal of promoting nation-building by deploying cadets away from their states of origin.

Fifth, the program must be well managed and well administered. This means getting a well-qualified staff and having a sound program of monitoring and evaluation.

Should cadets serve at home or away from home?
We suggest the choice of service location is a good area for a degree of decision-making by respective cadets. Claude Brown of the USA wrote in "Manchild in the Promised Land" that he wanted to become a better person but as long as he stayed in Harlem, he would be unable to resist the lure of the negative influences surrounding him. He moved away from Harlem and succeeded. By contrast, a number of young men from Harlem were posted by the Job Corps – a job training program for poor and unemployed young people started in 1964 as part of the War on Poverty -- to a rural area of Kentucky at about the same time and went out of control because they were unable to adjust to the very different environment. They returned to Harlem.

If cross-cultural experiences and a "melting pot" type of society are major goals of NYS, they will have a better chance of being met if cadets serve away from their homes and communities. Similarly, serving away from home will generally contribute more to Social Capital as cadets can be expected to interact with different kinds of people, and it will also give cadets a chance to satisfy their search for adventure and for finding themselves away from the influence of family and old friends.

At the same time, serving away from home makes the cadets more vulnerable to being influenced by the organization running NYS, especially if cadets live together as a group in barrack-like conditions. Such a situation facilitates political or ideological indoctrination, just as it does with boarding schools, summer youth camps, and the military services. However, it also permits the organization running NYS to provide a framework that enhances the cadets' opportunities for reflecting on their service experiences, hearing the viewpoints of cadets from other parts of the country and other socio-economic levels, and weighing the options open to them for further education and careers.

Should cadets serve on one project or more than one? We suggest that effective service delivery be the guiding rule in determining cadet activities. This usually means focusing on a single project. Most service activities require a certain level of skill and training; it takes several weeks to become proficient at the activity. In addition, many cadets are in human service positions where other persons are dependent on the cadets for caregiving or instruction and where the quality of service suffers from a rapid turnover of service providers. There are some exceptions. For example, cadets who serve as teacher aides during the school year might serve as playground or recreation aides during the summer months. Another exception might be found in tasks that are necessary but where the quality of service would not suffer from rapid turnover of cadets, e.g., cleaning litter from beaches and parks.

We recognize that a case can be made for multiple assignments where cadets benefit from experiencing different kinds of service and perhaps avoiding burnout or boredom. Good examples are found in Nigeria, New York City, and Canada. Cadets in Nigeria are expected to initiate part-time community development projects in addition to their primary assignments. Thus, a cadet who is a school teacher during the day may teach literacy classes to adults two or three nights a week. In addition, teams of cadets are assigned every April – when schools are on holiday -- to work on a labor-intensive project, usually in a rural area. They have built roads and bridges, community water tanks, and repaired schools and clinics.

In New York City, AmeriCorps cadets have two assignments during the year of service. One is in the physical services and the other in the human services. The idea is to expose the cadets to different areas of need in the city and to give them distinctly different kinds of experiences. During the 9-month Katimavik service period, cadets serve in three projects in three different parts of the country. This approach appears to benefit cadets more than those who are served.

Cadets gain different types of work experience and expand their networks of contacts for careers.

We have yet to see any research that is sufficiently rigorous to convince us which policy is best, but on balance, we think single project assignments are to be preferred.

What level of remuneration should a cadet receive? Salaries and benefits are issues both with military service and with NYS. At a minimum, there should be sufficient financial support to enable soldiers and cadets to have food, shelter and clothing. After the basic needs are covered, the questions arise, When does a volunteer soldier become a mercenary? And when does a volunteer cadet become an employee?

There is no uniform answer. Cadets serving in conservation programs and other services away from home are often given free housing and sometimes free food as well. Cadets with China's PARP usually receive the use of a bicycle while in service. Cadets who must provide their own food and accommodation often receive a stipend somewhat less than the minimum wage. Post-service benefits can also be found in many NYS programs. Many universities in the United States and elsewhere consider a prior service experience as adding to a candidate's qualification for admission.

In Israel, cadets who serve one year or longer receive a package of benefits at the end of their service. In 2004, these included $20 per month served; a deposit grant of about $90 per month served to be used for advanced education, buying a house, starting a business enterprise, or financing a wedding; and a special fund geared to the cadet's socio-economic status which may be used for such things as preparing for university entrance exams. The 30 percent of Sherut Leumi cadets who serve 21 months or longer are eligible for several additional benefits related to their employment status. Most employers have no legal requirements to hire former NYS cadets, but there is a tendency to prefer ex-cadets in recognition of their service contribution and because of their year or two of experience.

*   *   *   *   *

While certain practices are essential to the successful operation of NYS, it should be clear that we do not advocate a single ideal design for NYS. A country's history, its form of government, its geopolitical situation, and its resources are among the factors that will affect the design of NYS. What we do advocate is that countries and NGOs and educational institutions review the issues and recommendations raised in this chapter and make decisions on NYS appropriate to the respective country or institution.

CHAPTER 5

THE SPECIAL CASE OF SERVICE-LEARNING

Training for military service has always been based more heavily on experiential than on passive education. Following the introduction of universal education in many countries, experiential education was somewhat neglected. However, the latter decades of the 20th Century saw a swing back toward experiential education, particularly in the form of service-learning, which not only reinforces classroom education but delivers services to those in need and fosters the adoption of positive values by the students who serve.

A prelude to military service is found in the high schools and universities of many countries. Students learn how to march in formation, fire rifles, read maps, and generally become acquainted with matters military. The military services find it to be a useful source of educated military manpower, and many students find such experiences useful in deciding whether or not to pursue a military career.

Somewhat analogous to the military training in schools is a branch of NYS that has evolved throughout the world, especially in the years following World War II. Service-learning, as it is generally referred to, while found primarily in schools and universities, is also found increasingly in NYS programs. Unlike NYS, however, the background of service-learning is not linked to military service. Rather, its origins derive primarily from philosophers and politicians with ideas about educational reform.

Roots

Early in the 20th Century, Mahatma Gandhi criticized the elitism of the British system that had been imposed on India. He called for self-sufficient education in village schools throughout the country. Gandhi wanted children to learn crafts that would support them after leaving school, and ones that could be marketed to help pay for the cost of education.

In the 1960s Koesnadi Hardjasoemantri of Indonesia proposed Kuliah Kerja Nyata ("learning through real work") for universities in Indonesia. Hardjasoemantri, who wrote his doctoral dissertation on study-service, defined it as "students obtaining a very important part of their education by direct practical involvement in work which is of value to the welfare of other people and to the nation as a whole as well as to the development of their own personal integrity. (Hardjasoemantri, 1982) KKN became widely adopted by Indonesian universities in the 1980s but has since been cut back because of financial problems.

At about the same time in Tanzania, Julius Nyerere advocated "education for self-reliance," where every village school would be either a farm or a workshop, and where both teachers and students were also workers. In practice, however, schools failed to achieve the degree of integration sought by Nyerere. In 1971, a decade after the introduction of education for self-reliance, he wrote: "The fact is that we have a very long way to go before our educational policy is properly understood and properly applied…. We are still trying to graft working on to learning, as if the former is an extra being added to education just for the good of our souls." (Nyerere, 1992)

In Latin America, the concept of solidarity is at the heart of service-learning activities. Maria Nieves Tapia, the leader of service-learning in Argentina, says that "'Solidaridad' means helping others in an organized and effective way, means working together for the common cause, means standing as a group or as a Nation to defend your rights, to face natural disasters or economic crisis, and to do it hand in hand." (Tapia, 2002) Religion played a role in the evolution of service-learning in Latin America, where – especially in Roman Catholic schools – a voluntary or required service activity was seen as a manifestation of Christianity.

The solidarity concept was not limited to religious schools. In Cuba, when Fidel Castro in 1961 mobilized thousands of students for a literacy campaign, he admonished them with these words: "You are going to teach, but as you teach, you will also learn. You are going to learn much more than you can possibly teach, and in the end you will feel as grateful to the campesinos as the campesinos will feel to you for teaching them to read and write." (Eberly, 1978)

In North America early in the 20th Century interest in experiential education was generated by the writings of John Dewey on "learning by doing." Much of the "doing" that ensued proved to be a useful educational tool but was sterile from a societal point of view.

It was in the city of Atlanta in 1968 that the phrase service-learning was coined. A consortium of federal, regional, and local organizations put it this way: "It is [our] thesis that by combining the needs of society and resources of education both will be better served. It is hypothesized that the tension between the practical urgent demands of community and the requirements of disciplined rational thought of education can be a productive force for the development of society and for learning and the advancement of knowledge.

"This combination of action and reflection, of experience and examination, this integration of service and learning, can foster a style of life where education and ....vocation are parts of the same fabric and the gap between education and community is closed. Simply stated, then, service-learning is an integration of the accomplishment of a needed task with educational growth."(Atlanta Service-Learning Conference, 1970)

Europe lagged behind the rest of the world in service-learning. A 1970s survey of such programs identified the

United Kingdom as the only European country with such programs.   And they were the creation of Alec Dickson, originator of two NYS programs: Voluntary Service Overseas and Community Service Volunteers. (Pinkau, 1978)

It is good for NYS and service-learning to be linked conceptually because NYS administrators sometimes focus on the work to be done almost to the exclusion of exploiting the learning dimension of the experience. And the educators who usually run service-learning programs sometimes need reminding that the delivery of needed services is an essential element of the process.

A Balancing Act

All NYS cadets learn from their experiences in NYS, but their learning is enhanced when measures are taken to establish linkages between the service and the learning. Schools and universities have developed more highly structured service-learning experiences in cooperation with NGOs and public agencies. This is understandable when we consider that 200 years ago the education which young people acquired was about 99 percent experiential. The girls learned cooking from their mothers and the boys learned farming from their fathers or they learned trades as apprentices. Then the public schools came into being and young people were taught in classrooms. Then along came television and computers with the result that in many countries young people spend most of the day sitting down, both in classrooms and in front of the television or the computer screen.

We do not demean the learning found in the classroom or in front of the computer. But we do suggest as strongly as we can that a balance is needed between passive education and active education. Achieving that balance is a major aim of the service-learning programs in Indonesia, Costa Rica, India, and Mexico, cited in Chapter 3. Also, significant service-learning elements are found in a number of NYS programs designed for reasons other than service-learning. For example, members of

Volunteer Social Year in Germany are required to attend 25 seminar days during the course of the year for the purpose of enhancing the educational value of the service experience.

High school service-learning programs tend to be less productive in terms of service impact than full-time NYS. The students serve only a few hours per week and generally for only a few months. Still, the agencies where they serve are usually happy to have the students because they do provide some help, the patients and children and old people enjoy their company, and they are expected to become the volunteers of the future. Sometimes high school service-learning programs more than pay for their costs:

> In the village of Ramona, Argentina, eighth graders (age about 13) discovered in the school science laboratory that the water the villagers were drinking contained unacceptably high levels of arsenic. By the time they arrived in twelfth grade, they had ensured that their province provided their village with a drinking water plant, had the local administration build a new water system, and had organized (with the local hospital and two national universities) a health research and prevention system to treat people with symptoms of arsenic poisoning. (Maria Nieves Tapia as quoted in Gal, 2000)

Much of the learning acquired by the young people in Argentina, Costa Rica, Germany, Mexico, Nigeria, and the United States has been more indelible than that acquired in the classroom. From among these and other service-learning programs that have operated in various parts of the world, here are the principal outcomes of service-learning.

Outcomes

We know that the benefits of service-learning accrue to the person or persons served, to those individuals who serve, and to the wider community. A 2004 survey of a representative sample of school principals in the United States found that 30 percent of the schools engaged students in service-learning.

Among them, 90 percent reported that service-learning had a positive effect on students' civic engagement, personal and social development, and school-community relationships; and over 80 percent reported that it had a positive effect on the participating students' academic achievement. (Kielsmeier, 2004)

For example, in the American state of Minnesota, students in secondary school chemistry classes regularly monitor air and water pollution and make known their findings. The result is cleaner air and water for persons living in the immediate area of the high school, the award of academic credit to students for knowledge acquired from the process of measuring the pollutant levels in the air and water, and a small improvement to cleaner air and water over a much wider area.

Although large numbers of students participate in some service-learning programs, the nature of the experience is such that every person who participates in service-learning has a unique experience and derives a unique profile of values from the experience. Studies have revealed these major outcomes of service-learning:

• Increased awareness by participants of the needs of others;
• A better way to learn values than being lectured to;
• An effective way to reduce school violence;
• Increased levels of personal and social responsibility;
• More positive attitudes toward adults and others with whom they worked;
• Increased willingness to be active in one's community.

Service-learning is valuable for the message it sends to students, teachers, and the community. A school teaches values by its actions and policies, e.g., the money it spends on sports, theater, and driver education. A school that places service-learning in the curriculum and gives it adequate support sends the message to students that the school cares about the community and the environment.

Service-learning also acts as a prelude to full-time NYS. Although it cannot always be justified as a program in which services rendered exceed the cost, students do get acquainted with the challenges and rewards of serving others, they add to social capital by serving people of different ages and economic levels, and they get a good idea of the choices they want to make regarding entry into full-time NYS.

Service-learning can also have a profound impact on the way the adult members of a community view the younger members. Too often adults regard young people as trouble-makers. They view young people themselves as the problem. Here are some ways suggested by James Kielsmeier in which large-scale service-learning programs may be expected to change adult perceptions of young people.

From onlookers (especially via TV).....to active citizens
From apathetic ....to involved
From sheltered ....to shaper of society
From dependents ....to providers
From "at risk" ....to "at strength"

Principles

From years of observing service-learning programs, we recommend a set of ten principles.

1. Regard young people as an opportunity, not as a problem. Once we adopt this attitude and recognize young people as a largely untapped community resource, it becomes relatively easy to move toward the constructive involvement of young people in the community. A society that recognizes the unfilled potential of young people to serve and asks them to come forward to help will find them willing and perhaps eager to do so.

2. Welcome young people to the planning process for constructive community involvement. Young people crave experience. They are risk-takers and adventure-seekers. Much of what they do that adults regard as troublesome is simply young people's somewhat awkward groping for "real-life" experiences. They don't want to be told what to do, as perhaps they have been at home and at school; they want a voice in determining what they do.

3. Organize a survey of community needs.   High school students can work with teachers and others to design a community survey. Check with the agencies in City Hall, the churches, charitable organizations and elsewhere to determine the needs. Every community has old people who need help replacing light bulbs in the ceiling, repairing broken clotheslines, and a myriad of other small tasks so vital for daily life and yet so easy for teenagers to fix. Day-care centers and kindergartens need small chairs and tables and simple toys, all things that carpentry students can make.   Where there is heavy industry, neighboring residents often suffer from the effects of pollution. Chemistry students can monitor air and water pollution by testing samples in the laboratory. Physics students can check on noise pollution with audiometers.

The survey could be done tidily by adults but it is worth the extra effort to involve students under proper supervision. As well as assessing community needs, such a survey will also acquaint young people with potential service assignments, and potential supervisors with youthful volunteers. Those involved will acquire a fairly realistic sense of what to expect from the service-learning program.

It was just such a survey that gave impetus to the growth of service-learning in the United States in the 1970s. Student surveyors, working under the guidance of high school staff members, found that there would be enough service positions "to provide every 15- through 20-year-old in the areas surveyed with almost three hours of service-learning opportunities a week, some in jobs that require only a few hours each week, others in full-time work for a half year or more." (Havighurst, 1972)

4. Design the service-learning experience so as to offer promise of a successful experience by the service-learning participant. Success is important in building the participants' self-confidence. The main factors to watch for here are the level of competence and the duration of assignment. In order to grow, the participant should be asked to perform at a somewhat higher level than he has in the past, but the assignment must not be so difficult as to be impossible of accomplishment by the participant. Also, a one-to-one assignment should not be ended just as the service-learning participant gets to know the person he is working with. While some projects are never finished, there should be expectation of reasonable closure within the assigned period of time.

5. Be sure that the service part of a service-learning experience is a meaningful activity for the agency involved and is seen to be a meaningful activity by the participant. This means that the service-learning participant should usually play some role in project definition and in project assignment. Perhaps she will carry it out from conception to execution. More likely she will come in at a stage where the agency has a variety of briefly described positions, and the participant, in discussion with the agency officials, adds shape and substance to the activity she will undertake.

6. Give academic recognition for a service-learning experience on the basis of the learning acquired. not for performing a service. The evidence that learning has been acquired may be given in many forms: verbally, on paper, film, tape, graphically, artistically. The persons responsible for judging the award of credit should be associated with educational institutions. The American city of Atlanta requires all high school students to perform 75 hours of community service and to write an essay on the service experience and what was learned from it. Then, if the essay is judged as satisfactory and the students have met the other requirements for graduation, they are permitted to graduate.

7. Have a learning framework for the service experience before it begins. The framework can be developed in class sessions or in meeting individually with students. It should set forth the anticipated service activities together with a set of anticipated learning outcomes or of questions to be answered by the service experience. The framework should not be rigid; events during the course of the service may require it to be changed. The learning framework should extend throughout the service period and include these features:

•*A journal,* a daily account of one's service activities together with things that have been learned and questions raised by the service experience.
•*Periodic reflection sessions.* These are normally done weekly or biweekly with a group of 15 to 20 service-learning students. Students consult their journals to report on their activities, their learnings, and to raise questions. Necessary changes in the learning framework can also be made at this time.
•*A final report and recognition.* Students should give reports on what they have learned; the educational institution should recognize the learning through the award of academic credit or a certificate; and the organization where the student served should recognize the service by such means as hosting a luncheon or writing a thank you letter.

8. Integrate service-learning with the curriculum. Service activities can be meaningfully linked with every subject. Language and literature students can give individual tutoring to illiterates learning to read and write. History students can visit with lonely old folks and make their days brighter while the students receive a personal view of life in their country half a century earlier, one that may be at odds with what they read in their history books. Community Service Volunteers in Great Britain has produced a set of guidebooks to facilitate the incorporation of service-learning into the classroom. The guidebooks, under the generic title of

Community Links with the GCSE [General Certificate of Secondary Education], describe how teachers can integrate community service with the curriculum. These two projects are taken from the guidebook for science students:

•Look around your local area for evidence of pollution, take photographs of this evidence. Analyze the type of pollution and its effect upon the environment and suggest ways in which it could be alleviated. Present your findings and solutions to your local council Environmental Health Officer, and those responsible for the pollution.

•From your knowledge of dietary requirements, plan a three-day menu for either a pre-school child or an active teenager. Discuss your plans with a dietician or a health visitor and modify your menus if necessary. Carry out a survey to find if the children or young people in your area are eating a similar diet to that which you have devised. Make recommendations based on your findings.

9. Engage a service-learning coordinator. This is a pivotal position and is essential for a well-run service-learning process. The coordinator must be someone who understands community needs and can relate well to those involved in meeting them, who understands the educational interests of the school and can relate well to its administrators and teachers; and who understands the varied interests of the students, from those who seek constructive participation in the community to those who seek any excuse not to go to school.

Other duties of the service-learning coordinator are to be sure that there is adequate training, supervision, and transportation to and from the places of service. There may also be questions relating to accident coverage and legal liability that need to be resolved by the coordinator.

Service-learning programs often begin with someone serving in the position part-time. Usually that person is a teacher who is relieved of some of his teaching burden to work as the coordinator. Eventually, a secondary school of a few hundred or more students with a broad-based service-learning operation will require a full-time coordinator and possibly aides to the coordinator as well.

10. Find ways to involve out-of-school young people in service-learning. Many of them have found school an unpleasant experience and are unemployed because of their limited education. Still, there are a variety of service projects they can undertake. Many of them will be prepared to work full-time or nearly full-time. Consideration should be given to awarding them stipends for the services performed. As they serve, many of them will perceive the need for more education, particularly if it is tied in with their service activities.

*   *   *   *   *

It is worth remembering that young people are always involved in the community. The question is whether that involvement is constructive or destructive. A well-designed and operated program of service-learning increases the proportion of young people who are constructively involved in the community while strengthening the education and maturation of those young people.

CHAPTER 6

NATIONAL YOUTH SERVICE AS A PSYCHO-SOCIAL PROCESS

Veterans of military service sometimes refer to it as the best years of their lives. They say it helped them to mature, to discover themselves, to learn comradeship and cooperation. NYS also yields a range of psychological and social outcomes, a number of which parallel those in military service.

Discussions about NYS frequently mention the benefits to the individual, no less than the benefits to the community and the larger society. In analyzing the benefits to participants, however, we will focus in this chapter not only on the cadet's development as a good citizen nor, on the occupational aspects frequently stressed in such analyses. Instead, this chapter focuses on the psycho-social processes, or developmental processes, involved in serving in NYS.

Thus, we will first delineate the developmental parameters relevant to this youth activity; we will then describe the psychological characteristics of such youth service in general; finally, we will suggest what appear to be the main psycho-social impacts of voluntary youth work on its participants. It should be noted, however, that many young people do not participate in any form of youth service, yet they develop into healthy, balanced adults. Thus we know that the conditions for positive psycho-social development are neither specific nor limited to NYS.

Developmental Aspects

Several developmental aspects converge in the following discussion. First, the importance of *critical periods* in the development of an individual's personality should be explained. These are defined periods, "windows of time," during which certain kinds of exposures and experiences have a particularly strong impact. In the course of an individual's development there are several such "windows."

The classic example is described by Erik Erikson's model of eight stages of psycho-social development (Erikson, 1950; 1968). According to Erikson, the individual faces a life crisis in each stage of his/her psycho-social development. Such crises may have favorable or unfavorable outcomes, and the resolution of the life crisis will determine, for example, his/her ability to hope and trust in the future (as opposed to fear of the future and basic suspicion), to initiate activities, and to develop a sense of self-control and self-esteem.

Typically, NYS occurs, in terms of Erikson's model (See opposite page), at the end of the adolescence stage and the beginning of the early adulthood stage.   Favorable outcomes of formative experiences during these periods may include "the ability to see oneself as a unique and integrated person and to sustain loyalties," and "the ability to commit oneself, one's identity, to others" (Gardner, 1982).

While   Erikson's   model   still   gains   universal recognition, one can not ignore the vast changes that have occurred over the past half century, which have in turn altered the nature of psychological development in the late teens and early twenties for young people in industrialized societies. Because marriage and parenthood are delayed nowadays until the mid or late twenties for many people, it is no longer normative for the late teens and early twenties to be the phase of entering and settling into long-term adult roles.   On the contrary, these years are more typically a period of frequent change and exploration (Arnett, 1998; Rindfuss, 1991).

Subsequently,   several   authors   have   attempted,   in recent years, to 'adjust' Erikson's model to these recent changes. J.J. Arnett has (Arnett, 2000) proposed a new theory of development, focusing specifically on the ages of 18-25.

Figure 1: Erikson's Stages of Psycho-Social Development

Stage	Favorable Outcome	Unfavorable Outcome
First Year Trust – mistrust	Hope. Trust in environment and future	Fear of future; suspicion
Second Year Autonomy – shame, doubt	Will. A sense of self-control and self-esteem leading to good will and pride	Sense of loss and self control; a propensity for shame and doubt.
Third through Fifth Years Initiative – guilt	Purpose. Ability to initiate activities, and enjoy accomplishment	Fear of punishment; self-restriction or over compensatory showing off
Sixth Year through Puberty Industry – inferiority	Competence and skillfulness	A sense of inadequacy and inferiority
Adolescence Identity – Confusion about one's role	Fidelity. Ability to see oneself as a unique and integrated person and sustain loyalties	Confusion over who one is
Early Adulthood Intimacy – isolation	Love. Ability to commit oneself, one's identity, to others	Avoidance of commitments and of love; distancing of oneself from others
Middle Age Generativity – Stagnation	Care. Widening concern for one's children, work or ideas	Self-indulgence, boredom and interpersonal impoverishment.
Old Age Integrity – Despair	Wisdom. Assurance of the meaning of life; acceptance that one will die	Disgust with life; despair over death

Labeling this period **emerging adulthood**, Arnett is arguing that this developmental period is neither adolescent not youth adulthood but rather a distinct *critical period* by itself. It is "distinguished by relative independence from social roles and from normative expectations. Having left the dependency of childhood and adolescence, and having not yet entered the enduring responsibilities that are normative in adulthood, emerging adults often explore a variety of possible life directions in love, work, and world-views. Emerging adulthood is a time of life when many different directions remain possible, when little about the future has been decided for certain, when the scope of independent exploration of life's possibilities is greater for most people than it will be at any other period of the life course". (Arnett, 2000; p. 469).

It should be noted, however, that emerging adulthood is not necessarily a universal period, across cultures and socio-economical classes. Rather, it could be found, most likely, in countries that are highly industrialized or postindustrial; likewise, among developing countries, emerging adulthood will more probably characterize young individuals in urban areas, or in relatively higher socio-economic class.

These individuals typically marry later, become parents later and obtain more education than their counterparts in non-industrialized countries, or in lower socio-economic levels.

Whether applying Erikson's traditional scheme, or adapting more modern terminology, it is clear nevertheless that the period of NYS occurs within a critical transitional stage in the youth participants' lives.

A second developmental aspect relevant to our subject comes from a school of thought known as Existential Psychology. Abraham Maslow offered a unique perspective on psycho-social development which he framed in terms of *needs* rather than *chronology*. This is known as Maslow's "hierarchy of needs" (1968) (See opposite page). According to Maslow, there are five existential human needs, varying from the very fundamental (i.e. physiological and safety needs) through psycho-social needs, to the 'highest' needs of self-actualization. (In a later version, Maslow has added a *need for transcendence* - the experience of being able to see oneself in perspective – that is even higher than the need for self-actualization; Maslow, 1971).

Figure 2: Maslow's Hierarchy of Needs

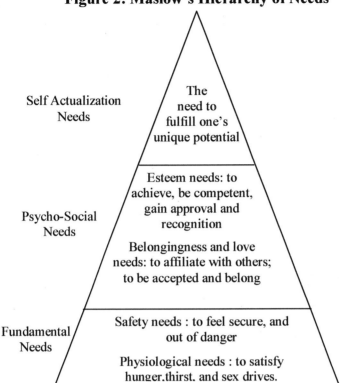

While Maslow's hierarchy of needs does not necessarily resemble chronological development (e.g. grown adults may still struggle fulfilling fundamental needs), it may reflect, nevertheless, periods in one's life of predominant wants. Looking from this perspective, we may conclude that young volunteers encounter the period of NYS at the stage of psycho-social needs, when fundamental needs have been satisfied, but self-actualization has not yet occurred (partly because the psychological needs have not yet been satisfied).

Among the psycho-social needs in Maslow's model are "esteem needs"—to achieve, to be competent, to gain approval and recognition, and the needs for love, acceptance and belonging. Only when these needs have been satisfied can a person begin to address the need for self-actualization.

Finally, another model of development refers to the age bracket of NYS as the "launching phase" (Duvall, 1985). This is when children leave their parental nest to exercise independence and autonomy – through college studies, military service, or overseas 'adventure trips' - even though they have not yet reached economic, social or even emotional independence. Typically, at this stage, youngsters would strive to perform "adult" tasks – while preserving the option of returning to the "safe nest" (Barnhill and Longo, 1978).

Psychological Characteristics of NYS

What are the characteristics of NYS (or any form of voluntary youth work), its framework and setting, that make it such a psychologically formative experience? It is a multi-part answer, some of which lies in the juxtaposition of seemingly contradictory processes and situations that offer a range of opportunities and challenges for personal growth:

> •*Independence.*   NYS frequently involves leaving home and engaging in situations and settings that allow-- indeed demand-- greater personal autonomy.
> •*Group Life*. Together with greater personal autonomy, NYS - by its inherent teamwork nature - requires the individual to take part in group efforts, to closely affiliate and interact with others and to identify with common goals.
> •*Coping with Difficulties*. NYS tasks and life conditions generate abundant challenges of unfamiliar situations, pressure and sometimes significant mental stress.
> •*Opportunities for Success and Accomplishment*. Along with the difficulties, the NYS period is frequently characterized by successful achievements and opportunities for accomplishment.

The other part of the answer is found in the opportunities for constructive personal growth that are frequently encountered by the average NYS cadet.

•Focus on Altruism. NYS allows the cadet to focus on actions of giving and providing, and on attentiveness to others.

•Appreciation and Reinforcement. Typically, the mere nature of NYS activities results in frequent opportunities for the cadet to receive expressions of gratitude and appreciation, esteem and meaningful affirmation by others.

•Grown-up Expectations. The NYS period is predominately characterized by the demand on the cadet to assume responsibility and make decisions, to fulfill expectations and obligations, and to exercise self-discipline while serving the needs of children, adults, or the elderly. The young cadet is frequently called upon to function as a responsible adult in inter-generational settings, and sometimes as a figure of authority. This experience stands in stark contrast to the "moratorium" period during which young persons in industrialized societies typically postpone responsibilities and functions, sometimes until the age of thirty.

•Gender Interaction. NYS is a period characterized by mutual acquaintance between the sexes, in the context of joint action, mutual support, and personal revelation. Unlike the casual, ritualized meetings between the sexes in pubs, discotheques, etc., the encounter between

the sexes in the framework of NYS is a process
of on-going discovery, without facades or
posturing.

These are some of the universal characteristics of NYS.
Intensive exposure to these opportunities and challenges over
the course of a year or more, during a critical period in the
cadet's psycho-social development, often results in extremely
significant and usually quite apparent transformations in the
personal identity of young men and women. Everyone who
has been involved a long time with NYS volunteers has been
struck by the apparent impact that such a period of NYS-type
service has on volunteers' personality, attitudes, maturity and
identity.

The Psycho-Social Effects of NYS

Empirical research about the impact of voluntary
service is relatively scarce. However, two reports have been
found which are relevant to this discussion. The first extensive
report is that of the AmeriCorps (Corporation for National
Service, 1997). This evaluation report (conducted by an
external agency) includes evaluations of outcomes and
impacts of two AmeriCorps cohorts (1994-5 and 1995-6) on
both beneficiaries (communities, organizations and individuals
served by AmeriCorps volunteers), and on cadets. The latter
comprises four areas of member impacts: life skills, civic
responsibility, educational attainment, and educational
opportunity.

Pertinent to our specific subject is the 'life-skills'
category, comprising interpersonal skills, communication,
problem-solving, etc. Over 40 percent of participants reported
"gaining a lot" in these areas as a result of their year of
service. Another 20-30 percent reported that they had gained
"a little." It should be noted that these 'psychological' gains
were substantially higher than reported gains in other life-skill
areas, such as "understanding organizations" or "using

information technology."   As summarized by the report editors, these "sorts of skill growth.... are those broad foundation skills which play a role in virtually every domain of interpersonal functioning in a high-performance society and economy". (1997: p. 117).

The second example of a systematic evaluation of a voluntary youth service is that of the Canadian NYS, Katimavik (1999). While quite different from the AmeriCorps in its structure and goals (Katimavik volunteers are divided into groups of 12 youths of which half are females, half are males, one third are Francophones and two thirds are Anglophones, representing every Canadian region as well as various social and economic backgrounds), the reported psychological impact on the Katimavik participants following 9 months of voluntary work bears very similar results: About 40-50 percent of the respondents in the evaluation study indicated improved skills as team members, in interpersonal communication and in leadership – as a result of their Katimavik experience. In their summary, the authors stress that "although participants have noted a significant improvement of their psychological skills, they have identified the main benefits of Katimavik in terms of maturing: self-knowledge, attitudes and behavior towards others..." (1999, p. 4).

> In Canada in 1985, I visited a Katimavik House in Montreal where 12 Katimavik members lived with their group leader. It was part of a nine-month total life experience, during which time the group lived in Katimavik Houses in three different parts of the country where they participated in three service projects, spent two weeks individually with families whose primary language was different from theirs, and had domestic responsibilities ranging from cleaning to shopping to preparing meals (DJE).

Based on these reports and even more on observations, personal communications and accumulated impressions from

NYS programs around the world[2], here are some of the most typical psychological and inter-personal outcomes of participating in a volunteer youth service:

• *A Sense of Citizenship and Affiliation.* NYS shapes and strengthens the cadet's sense of citizenship, solidarity and engagement in the commonweal. Graduates of NYS programs frequently report that it was through their voluntary work that they came to understand the principle of civic duty and that the service period had fostered and strengthened their personal sense of duty and social responsibility.

• *Self Confidence and Self-Efficacy.* NYS cadets normally develop their self-confidence and the faith in their own ability to accomplish tasks and missions not previously within their scope of achievement. This is exactly what Albert Bandura meant in his "self-efficacy" concept. (1977, 1982). According to Bandura, self-efficacy is important to personality development because it greatly affects whether or not a person will even try to accomplish challenging tasks. The NYS period provides many opportunities for its participants to try – and often to successfully accomplish – such tasks.

• *Locus of Control.* This concept grew in recent years out of social-psychology theories dealing with the person- situation interaction. The internal - external dimension of Locus of Control defines an individual's generalized belief about the source of causality and control over events. Individuals with an *internal* locus of control are more likely to believe that events and outcomes are consequences of their own behavior, whereas individuals with an *external* locus of control tend to see outcomes and consequences as less dependent on their own actions and more dependent on other people or on

[2] A crucial source of information here are the biennial Global Conferences organized by the International Association of National Youth Service (IANYS).

chance. (Rotter, 1966; 1975). Evidently the experience of NYS enhances in its participants an internal locus of control, hence generating in them a sense of mastery over circumstances and their consequences. For young persons, this is a very powerful state-of-mind with which to launch into adult life.

• *Leadership.* All of the above outcomes enable young NYS cadets to realize their leadership potential. Psychological maturity, social skills and the situational opportunities of NYS combine to create the conditions of leadership; namely, confidence in one's ability to influence others, to set goals and achieve them, and to enlist others in one's vision.

• *Social and Emotional Intelligence.* In recent years, the notion that there are different forms of intelligence has evolved dramatically (e.g. Gardner, 1983). Furthermore, it has been confirmed that unlike 'basic' intelligence that is merely genetically determined, other forms of intelligence are affected by experience and development (Sternberg, 1990). Evidently, the NYS experience can contribute to the development of what is currently termed "social and emotional intelligence." While the former has been traditionally conceptualized in terms of interpersonal astuteness and social adaptation (Endler and Summerfeldt, 1995), emotional intelligence has been defined as "a subset of social intelligence that involves the ability to monitor one's own and other's feelings and emotions, to discriminate among them, and to use this information to guide one's thinking and actions." As he/she learns to adapt to new and unfamiliar situations, in contact with a broad range of people who may differ in age, background, and beliefs, the NYS participant develops the capacity for empathy, non-verbal awareness both of self and of others, and a sense of the commonality of the human condition. Such traits enable the healthy and mature person to recognize and accept complex realities and to function effectively within them.

• *Sexual Maturity.* Such a nuanced approach contributes not only to a healthy social personality but also to a healthy sexual maturity. Young men and women experience their peers of the opposite sex in NYS as multi-faceted partners, co-workers, and friends. Thus, their sexual identity and attitudes may avoid objectification of themselves and others as sexual objects; rather, they are likely to develop respectful attitudes towards the other sex, along with a healthy sense of attractiveness and desirability.

Returning to our earlier discussion of Erikson's and Arnett's developmental models, the following effects of voluntary service were also observed:

Independent Identity. In Erikson's terms, the formation of an independent identity that is both unique and integrated is one of the favorable outcomes of the Adolescence period.

Sustained Loyalty. Again in Erikson's terminology, this is the ability to sustain loyalty to others, including friends, community, and society, as well as loyalty to oneself – in terms of one's values, faith and an articulated world-view.

Commitment. The ability to invest energy and effort in a sustained commitment to oneself and to others.

Generosity and sense of giving. The nurturing of altruism, generosity of spirit, and giving of oneself to others is one of the most prevalent outcomes of an intensive involvement in NYS. This stands in contrast to trends of competition, self-centeredness and "self-fulfillment," which are so normative in modern   society.

*   *   *   *   *

The rise of intolerance, inter-ethnic conflict and alienation in virtually every corner of our planet teaches us that NYS still has an important role to fill. In a world where the young are frequently seen as a problem, to open for them programs of voluntary service is to believe in their energy, their capabilities and their determination to positively influence the course of change in terms of a better future. (Ferreira, 2000). The structure and essence of NYS offer uniquely intensive, constructive and appropriate conditions—ideal for nurturing active citizens, empathetic neighbors, and adults with an integral and inclusive world-view. NYS not only materializes such potential. It creates it.

PART III

THE IMPACT OF NATIONAL YOUTH SERVICE

The power of the NYS idea is found in its impact on those who serve, on those who are served, and on the communities and nations where they serve. In short, NYS is a strong policy worthy of consideration in all countries.

CHAPTER 7

THE SERVICE IMPACT OF NATIONAL YOUTH SERVICE

Military service came into being not for the benefit of the soldiers but for the results it would produce, whether to defend the nation or to conquer other lands. Service delivery is always a vital part of NYS, and often the activities of cadets are as arduous as those in military service. But where Chapter 6 notes a number of similarities in the impact on the individual of military service and NYS, the service impacts of NYS are quite unlike those of military service.

Few countries do a benefit/cost analysis of NYS programs. It is impossible to do in the short-term because many of the benefits are long-term. And longitudinal studies are very expensive. But a number of studies have been made of the value of services rendered. The most rigorous of these show a benefit/cost ratio of between 1:1 and 2:1, with urban services in the higher range and conservation services in the lower. Reports from different parts of the world illustrate the range and magnitude of NYS impacts.

NYS Impact Studies

A report on the first 20 years of Nigeria's NYSC describes the impact in major service areas. Some 70 percent of the 400,000 cadets who served during that period were in the field of education where they contributed substantially, especially in the more remote areas of Nigeria. In the field of health, each local government area received at least two qualified health personnel such as doctors, dentists, and pharmacists. NYSC cadets also contributed to rural infrastructure by organizing community projects to build roads, bridges, and landscaping. In agriculture, cadets cultivated at least 100 hectares of land in each of the 30 states, producing a large amount of corn, rice, cassava, and pineapples. Also, necessity led to a number of inventions by cadets, from a potato thresher to a phototherapy set to a multi-purpose textile drying machine. (Enegwea and Umoden, 1993)

The large-scale impact of the NYSC continues into the 21st Century. Between 2000 and 2003, more than 300,000 cadets in Nigeria's NYSC had received instruction on reproductive health and HIV/AIDS. Of that number, 15,000 had become trainers of peer educators and each of them had trained about 40 young people as peer educators. Thus, some 600,000 young people had become peer educators over the course of three years. Although it is not known how many other young people they reached, the fact that nearly one million young people had become well informed about HIV/AIDS seemed certain to have a dampening effect on the spread of that disease in Nigeria. (Oki, 2004)

A 2002 study found that Canada's Katimavik elevated the quality of 92 percent of the projects on which cadets worked, and successfully met the project's goals on 68 percent of the projects. In assessing the total economic impact of Katimavik, the study found that it was 49 percent greater than Katimavik's budget. The study also found that the program had a marked impact on the career paths of cadets: 67 percent of NYS cadets chose a career path as a direct result of the Katimavik experience whereas only 14 percent of a control group of non-cadets chose a career path in the same time frame. (Etude Economic Conseil, 2002)

Enrollment in India's National Service Scheme early in the 21st Century was about two million in any one year. In one project, some 1,800 acres of wasteland was made useful by involving 11,000 cadets over a five-year period. Large numbers of cadets have also been involved in awareness programs related to HIV/AIDS, drug abuse, consumer protection, human rights, voting rights, and environmental protection. Other areas of service delivery include soil testing and crop clinics, construction of smokeless hearths, digging of ponds for water conservation, planting of saplings, and literacy education. (Nagar, 2004)

The primary impact of the Ghana National Service Scheme (GNSS) is in the field of education. From 1990 until 2002, 65 percent of the NYS cadets served as teachers and tutors, especially in the poor villages of northern Ghana. An indication of the service impact is given by the fact that the allowances received by cadets are somewhat less than half the amount they would receive as salaried teachers. (Akoto-Danso, 2004) In addition to education, the GNSS operates several demonstration projects in the areas of health and the environment.

> In 2004, I visited the Papao Demonstration Farm that had been established by the GNSS in the 1980s as an ecologically friendly, self-sustaining farm, and that is maintained by National Service personnel. No commercial fertilizers are used and they grow rice, cassava, coconuts, plantains, oranges, palm nuts, corn, onions, and other fruits and vegetables. They keep pigs, goats, chickens, and maintain several ponds for raising fish. They keep beehives for the production of honey and they make soap and kente cloth. School groups and village groups are frequent visitors to the farm. It is a model that might well be replicated in other NYS programs. (DJE)

A 2001 study of NYS in Israel took into account not only the stipends and other cadet-related payments; it also put opportunity costs, a temporary loss of return on education, and other such costs into the benefit/cost equation. Benefits were comprised almost entirely of the value of services received by those who were served. The result of the study of just over 20,000 cadets in assorted NYS programs was a benefit figure of $US296 million, and a cost figure of $US262 million, or a benefit/cost ratio of 1.13. (Fleischer, 2004)

> In Israel in 2000 I met a group of about half a dozen young women doing a year of NYS as members of Shlomit. They were serving as teacher aides and tutors in an elementary school with both Arab and Jewish students. One of the women was Arab and the others were Jews. At another site I met a member of Shlomit who was an ambulance aide, the only person in the ambulance besides the driver.(DJE)

The impact of NYS in Europe is illustrated by the rise in the number of cadets in non-conscription related programs such as Germany's Voluntary Social Year (VSY). During the decade from 1993-2003, the number rose from 11,500 to some 44,000. In 1990, only Germany had a government-regulated long-term voluntary service, and by 2004 they were found as well in Austria, the Czech Republic, Italy, and Luxembourg; while they were being considered in Estonia, the Netherlands, and the UK. (Stringham, 2004)

The major impact of NYS in Argentina, as it is in much of Latin America, is found in service-learning. From a virtually unknown type of pedagogy in the early 1990s, by 2004 service-learning projects were found in some 5,000 schools and 100 universities. Service-learning was launched by the Ministry of Education in 1997 but was interrupted in 2002 as a result of the economic and political crisis. This led to the creation of the Center for Service-Learning in Latin America (CLAYSS) in 2002 that picked up the ball from the Ministry and extended its outreach throughout Latin America. Service-learning is a manifestation of solidarity. The students express solidarity with people in need by helping them out, and officials of the public agencies and NGOs where the students serve show their solidarity with the students by welcoming them and providing support services. (Elicegui, 2004)

A cost/benefit analysis of AmeriCorps showed that for every US$1 spent the country receives US$1.66 in return. According to their 1995 measure, direct benefits alone exceeded total program costs. (Aguirre, 1997) These results were consistent with the national service experiment conducted by the

United States government in Seattle in 1973-74 (See Chapter 4). The host agencies valued the work done by cadets at double the cost of the program to the federal government. The unemployment rate among cadets fell from 70 percent at entry to 18 percent six months after completion of service. Two-thirds of cadets reported that the NYS experience had influenced their career or educational plans, and 25 percent said they had received or expected to receive academic credit for evidence of their learning acquired from the NYS experience. In a nationally-normed test of career development for which the norm was one step up the career ladder during the course of one year, the cadets averaged two steps up the ladder. (Kappa Systems, Inc. 1975)

For an industrial country, the Seattle test is a good indicator of the kinds of service positions young people might fill in an urban area if given the opportunity:

Distribution of Seattle Cadets

Education 25%
Social Services...23
Mental Health..11
Crime and Protection.....................................10
Recreation...10
Health Services... 9
Employment Services.......................................6
Other...6

In order to account for an estimated 15 percent of cadets who would serve in conservation and environmental activities outside urban areas, the above figures would decline proportionally. In a non-industrial country, there would likely be greater proportions of cadets serving in the areas of health, education, and agriculture.

These projects are typical of NYS activities worldwide. The basic idea is that the work done by cadets either extends the outreach of or improves the quality of services rendered by the host organization, which is typically a non-governmental organization (NGO) or a public agency of the local, state, provincial, or central government. However, countries with low rates of GNP per capita often include activities that would be considered the domain of the private sector in countries with higher rates of GNP per capita. Thus, the construction of railways in China, the packaging of tea in Cuba, and the installation of a water system in Indonesia.

Also, cadets sometimes move directly into paid employment continuing their service work. What happens is that charitable projects, wherever they may be found, seldom are able to meet all the needs because of limited staff. So there are always plenty of things to do. When budgets permit, it is natural that they would look first to persons they know can do the job.

> In the United States in 1973 I met a young woman in Seattle who was mentally retarded and was doing NYS in a nursing home where she played games with residents and visited with them. Later I learned that after the year of service the residents and their families found her so helpful that they petitioned to have her kept on and she was hired to continue her work as an employee. (DJE)

Committed Service

Just as soldiers find combat to be intense, challenging, and perhaps exhilarating, the same is true of cadets in many NYS assignments. It is found especially in day care centers for pre-schoolers, in institutions caring for the mentally ill and mentally disabled, and in nursing homes for old people, as illustrated in this account by the parent of a cadet in Germany's Zivildienst.

> I have a son who is doing his service in the sick ward of an old people's home.... I asked him how many deaths he actually had witnessed during his one-and-a-half years of civilian service. He told me that he could no longer count them; but, on an average, there were more than one every

month. And you must bear in mind what it means to a young person who has just graduated from secondary school to take care of old people -- to wash and feed them, make their beds, care for them, help them up when they have fallen down and are bleeding, go for help when one of them has a stroke -- and then, at the end, watch the people, with whom he has just established contact, die. I ask myself the meaning of such arguments as the one that "military service is a greater strain," and I wonder what justification there actually is for making conscientious objectors do service for a period of time that is one-third longer than military service. (Quoted in Kuhlmann, 1990).

The observation of Professor of Psychiatry Hans R. Huessy helps to explain the effectiveness of cadets in a number of stressful situations. He describes the unique contribution that full-time volunteers can make: "The chronically disabled require a constant giving... and cannot give back in nearly equal amounts. Professionals who genuinely try, 'burn out.' They cannot sustain it.... Voluntary service is needed because there is no other way to meet the needs of these individuals that would be humane.... Professional consultation without caring does not work. Caring without professional input does not work. The professional input can be bought. The caring comes only through committed service." (Huessy, 1988)

*   *   *   *   *

NYS cadets from various socio-economic levels performing a wide range of services in different parts of the world render services valued at more than program costs. Also, it seems likely that the worth of benefits received by cadets over time from their service experiences exceeds the value of their contributions. Once the necessary longitudinal and comparative research is undertaken and publicized, the public and the policy-makers will be better able to chart the future course of NYS.   .

CHAPTER 8

YOUTH SERVICE AS STRONG POLICY

By Michael Sherraden

Governments and the societies they serve benefit from policies which produce multiple benefits. One example is military service. It is useful not only to defend a nation and to project its interests worldwide; it also helps to build a nation through the involvement of young people from all walks of life, and gives educational and maturational benefits to the soldiers. NYS is another example of what Michael Sherraden refers to as strong policy.

An earlier version of this chapter was written for the Worldwide Workshop on Youth Involvement as a Strategy for Social, Economic, and Democratic Development, sponsored by the Ford Foundation, San Jose, Costa Rica, January 4-7, 2000. Support for writing the paper has been provided by the Ford Foundation. The author is grateful to Vicente Espinoza, David Gillespie, Michael Lipsky, Amanda Moore McBride, Mark Schreiner, Margaret Sherraden, Susan Stroud, and participants at the workshop for comments and suggestions.

By the words strong policy I mean policy that has many positive impacts and provides an exceptional return on investment. Most people would agree that such a policy, if it can be identified, should be enacted and implemented.[3] But what are the characteristics of a strong policy? Is youth service a strong policy?

As an academic who has studied youth service, I am somewhat reluctant to admit that knowledge about youth service is lagging far behind public interest and political support. This is certainly true in the United States, and as far as I can tell, in many other countries as well. Unfortunately, theoretical understanding and empirical evidence to support youth service are only weakly developed. We have undertaken a number of studies over the years, but the thinking and research are still rudimentary. A great deal more knowledge about youth service will be necessary if we are to establish an adequate foundation to support major policy initiatives around the world. This chapter offers suggestions for how knowledge building for application might be most productive. In order to do this, I must first step briefly into matters of inquiry structure in the applied social sciences, and I hope the reader will bear with me. As will become evident, my purposes are entirely practical, and speak directly to policy development in youth service. Below I attempt to specify what a strong policy is from the viewpoint of the applied social sciences. Next, building on previous research, I elaborate on what strong policy means vis-à-vis youth service. Finally, I suggest directions for youth service research and policy.

Foundations of Policy Innovation

What are the foundations of strong policy -- policy that is clearly worth public and legislative support? This is a big

---

[3] David Gillespie cautions: "Your idea of strong policy seems to be similar to those looking for big effects, dramatic cures, etc. This could blind us to the small, strategically placed interventions that in time make huge differences." This warning is well taken, but it is probably not an either/or issue. Applied social researchers can look for big effects and also for small and long-lasting effects.

question, and I do not pretend to have a complete answer to it, but over many years I have developed some thinking that has been useful in guiding my work on the academic side of policy innovation. Based on this experience, allow me to suggest some principles.

Structure and action

The economist James Duesenberry once observed that "economics is about how people make choices, and sociology is about how people do not have any choices that they can make." This insightful comment captures the central tension in the social sciences -- between structure and action. Economics has focused on action by individuals (agency) and sociology has focused on structure (society). But this dichotomy misleadingly suggests that we must opt for either social structure or individual action. In fact, the most interesting questions in the applied social sciences are on that fertile ground where structure and action interact. The primary goal of social policy (a purposefully created structure) should be not to restrict or limit action, but to promote it. Along these lines, Adlai Stevenson once said of President Woodrow Wilson: "He taught us to distinguish between governmental action that takes over functions formerly discharged by individuals, and governmental action that restores opportunity for individual action" (in Latham, 1958).[4] To complete this thought, governmental action should restore opportunities for action at all levels -- individuals, families, associations, organizations, communities, and society as a whole. Any policy innovation in the social arena should be put to this simple and fundamental test.

---

[4] I am grateful to Donald Eberly for finding this quote.

Ideas before programs

First, policy innovators must have well-developed ideas, not merely program proposals. Second, ideas must be specified as theoretical statements – in the best case, logical and relatively simple theory, with clear and testable hypotheses. For policy purposes, we need very simple models that are productive (Krugman, 1995). Third, the causal variable(s) in these hypotheses must be translated into policy and program applications. If these conditions are present, then the policy innovator will know what she is proposing, what the program is supposed to accomplish, and what to measure in evaluation. To sum up these points: theory matters. It is an unfortunate misconception that applied social research can be or should be atheoretical. There is a notion, too common in applied social research, that dozens or hundreds or even thousands of empirical studies that are not based in theory will add up to something. In the absence of specific ideas that are being tested, data tend not to add up to anything. We end up with piles of information but little understanding. If an idea is well specified theoretically, policy and program implications will follow, and research can be productive in building knowledge (Sherraden, 1998).[5]

Clear and consequential ideas

Ideas for policy and practice should be simple, clear, logically constructed, thoughtful, and almost intuitively sensible. A

---

[5] Notwithstanding the current popularity of post-modern, non-positivist inquiry, the discussion in this paper assumes deductive positivism as the preferred epistemology for applied social research. In other words, the researcher should be aiming for theoretical statements that are testable. The tests can include many different types of research methods, both quantitative and qualitative, but the fundamental point is that theory is required. If the applied scholar does not know what the policy or other intervention is expected to accomplish (i.e., if there is no theory), there is no rationale for the intervention, and it is ethically very questionable (Sherraden 2000).

good test is whether the idea (distinct from the program description) can be communicated in a few sentences so that most people will understand it. If this is not the case, the thinking may not be clear enough to serve as a guide for action. To illustrate, in other work I have proposed that policy should promote asset accumulation among impoverished and excluded populations (Sherraden, 1991a). This would be a departure from the primary policy of income support in the "welfare states." Now, there are many complex questions regarding how assets are so unevenly distributed (e.g., Oliver and Shapiro, 1995), how people save (Beverly and Sherraden, 1999), and what the effects of asset accumulation might be (e.g., Yadama and Sherraden, 1996), but the basic notion of asset accumulation is remarkably simple, connecting directly with the experience and understanding of most people. Partly for this reason, asset building has in a relatively short period of time taken hold in the policy process (Sherraden, 2001).[6] I am wondering to what extent simplicity and clarity of ideas might be missing in many policy proposals that fail to engage the public's imagination.[7]

For the purposes of application, all ideas are not of equal value -- some have far greater potential in application than others. How are we to know a consequential idea when we see one?[8] This is a big question, and by no means do I

---

[6] The leadership of the Ford Foundation has been a key factor in asset building policy and program development in the United States.

[7] Often ideas that are not clear do not really have substance behind them. Also, unclear ideas can lead to vague policies, which invite confusion and abuse.

[8] This comment on the differential value of ideas does necessarily apply to the social sciences in general, because it may not be easy to know what a good basic research question is. However, the applied social sciences have a distinctive demand: application. In this context, if an idea is unlikely to have an impact, what is the point? Unfortunately, judgments regarding usefulness of ideas in the applied social sciences are too seldom made. Research tends to be evaluated more on methodological soundness than on whether the question is worth asking to start with.

have a complete answer to it, but I have come to view some inquiry structures as superior to others for the purposes of the applied social sciences. My point here is that the form of the inquiry matters, separate and apart from its theoretical specification or content.[9]

To approach this reasoning, allow me to begin with what I think is not very a good in inquiry structure for the applied social sciences. In unfortunate but very familiar cases, we find studies with a dozen or more potential causes (independent variables) looking for effects on a single outcome (dependent variable). What is wrong with this? Most studies that rely on this many-independent-variable-and-single-dependent-variable structure are of limited use in terms of action guidelines because, typically, no single independent variable accounts for enough of the variance in the dependent variable to make much of a difference, and therefore applied implications are few.[10] Even if a single independent variable accounted for 10 percent of the variance, which is not common in social research, seldom would a decision be made to invest in something that predicts only 10 percent of the outcome of interest. Interventions are expensive, and rarely would or should an intervention be undertaken to target only a small percentage of the variance in a dependent variable.[11]

---

[6] That the form of the inquiry structure is influential apart from specification and content perhaps has something in common with Marshall McLuan's (1994) famous phrase regarding the communications media: "The medium is the message."

[10] David Gillepsie raises the possibility that my discussion of inquiry structures may confuse statistical theory with substantive theory. Outcomes of statistical theory are only one way to inform the value of substantive theory, and the amount of variance explained cannot be taken as the actual strength of the substantive relationship. While this is technically accurate, substantive theory is very often tested statistically, and the statistical test is usually the best information we have.

[11] This may be overstated. Mark Schreiner suggests that there may be cases where a policy investment should be made even if it affected only a

A desirable alternative is to turn the structure around, wherein a theoretical statement has one independent variable and multiple dependent variables. I have come to think of this as working with a "strong independent variable," one that has many positive effects. If a single independent variable can be shown to have desirable effects across a broad range of dependent variables, even if each effect is quite modest, then it would sometimes make sense to "intervene" by altering this single variable.[12] For example, if an independent variable accounted for an average of four percent of the variance of eight different dependent variables, all in a desirable direction, then this independent variable might be a good candidate for policy innovation.[13] For example, this is the inquiry structure for propositions on multiple effects of tangible assets mentioned above (Sherraden, 1991a). This would seem to be a constructive way for applied social researchers and policy innovators to think, because changing one variable can potentially have many positive impacts.[14]

---

few percentage points of the outcome of interest. In my view these situations are likely to be uncommon.

[12] It is likely that if an independent variable has many positive effects, it also has some negative effects. Theorists and researchers should of course search for all relevant effects, positive and negative.

[13] Melvin Oliver, in introducing this presentation at the Costa Rica meeting, emphasized that the variance explained on a given dependent variable is likely to be quite modest. The strength of this reasoning is that there might be multiple effects, even if all quite modest, which together might represent a meaningful impact. As a caveat, the multiple dependent variables would have to be statistically independent, i.e., have low intercorrelations, in order to claim multiple effects from the independent variable.

[14] This discussion assumes direct effects models that are typical in social research. In dynamic models it may that a different type of conceptual device is the key to theory for application. Positive feedback loops are a likely candidate. David Gillespie suggests that applied social research should move in this direction. This suggestion is intriguing, but it is a large and complex topic that must wait for another day.

Structures of Inquiry in the Applied Social Sciences

Let us put this suggestion in a somewhat larger context. To greatly oversimplify, we can identify four types of inquiry structures in the applied social sciences. These are illustrated in their simplest form in Figure 1 and described below. The types are intended, in the simplified way, to capture main characteristics, on which there can be many, many variations. I do not intend this to be an exhaustive classification – there are other possibilities – but these four inquiry forms can represent the vast majority of applied social research. Two dimensions are employed in sorting out types of inquiry structure: focus on a negative vs. focus on a positive, and explanation vs. impact (Figure 1).

First, I distinguish between constructs that are typically considered to be negative vs. constructs that are typically considered to be positive ("problems" vs. "successes") because this is in fact how most work in the applied social sciences is formulated. In the best social science, constructs are continuous and would range from the very positive to the very negative, so this idea of "problems" vs. "successes" would not be relevant, and indeed would often represent sloppy thinking (Hage, 1972). But as a practical matter, applied social science is not this pristine and scholars most often are dealing with something that they think of as a problem or, alternatively, something that they think of as a success. Problem-oriented studies account for most inquiry in the applied social sciences. As rough estimates, I would guess that problem-oriented inquiries, implicit or explicit, represent 90-95 percent of applied psychological research, 80-90 percent of public health research, 80-90 percent of social work research, 60-80 percent of applied sociological research, and 50-75 percent of applied economics research. The general assumption is that if we better understand a problem (either its explanation or its impact) we will be able to do something about it. This assumption sounds quite reasonable, but unfortunately it is often misplaced. Most problem-oriented research does not result in clear policy or practice implications. If I had to point to a single factor that most limits the applied social sciences it would be the pervasive focus on problems.

Much less common is a focus on positive constructs or "successes." This distribution of prevalence of types of inquiry seems odd when one stands back and thinks about it. Why are the applied social sciences so preoccupied with problems? Perhaps because it is easier to detect influences on problems than to identify solutions. It might be helpful to ask more often, in the explanatory mode, "how do people succeed?" instead of the usual question, "how do people fail?" In the impact mode, theory and research might examine not so much the effects of problems as the effects of positive interventions: What can be done that will make a positive difference?[15]

The second dimension, explanation vs. impact, separates studies that employ many independent variables to explain one dependent variable from studies that attempt to show the impact of one independent variable upon many dependent variables. This is not to say that inquiry can prove causality, which is extraordinarily difficult to do, but only that causality is implied in theoretical statements. Explanation

---

[15] This is not an original viewpoint; many others have questioned the excessive focus on problems. For example, in the area of youth policy, the movement toward "positive youth development" is a well-justified reaction to decades of problem-oriented youth research and policy. More broadly, one can point to the "strengths perspective" in social work practice, which has arisen in recent years in response to a perceived excessive focus on problems (e.g., Weick et al., 1989; Saleeby, 1997). While there is not space here for an extended critique, a major shortcoming of these more positive approaches is lack of theory. As they stand, "positive youth development" and the "strengths perspective" are more ideological statements than guides to inquiry.

comes in many forms, the most common represented by multiple regression statistical methodology wherein the explanatory power of numerous independent variables can be sorted out. As a rough estimate, I would say that 80-90 percent of applied social research is in the explanation form.[16] On the other hand, the impact form represents the typical "problem analysis" or "policy analysis," wherein a construct of interest is assessed in terms of its effects or impacts on multiple dependent outcomes.

If we put these simple classifications into a table of possible types, we have four different inquiry structures (illustrated in Figure 1). Applied social researchers tend to operate in one of these modes or another.

EXPLANATION	IMPACT
I. Explanation of a Negative FOCUS ON A NEGATIVE	**II. Impact of a Negative**
III. Explanation of a Positive FOCUS ON A POSITIVE	**IV. Impact of a Positive**

Figure 1. Some Types of Inquiry Structures in the Applied Social Sciences

---

[16] One cannot help but wonder to what extent the preponderance of explanatory studies is due to readily available statistical methodologies – regression, analysis of variance, path analysis -- that assume this inquiry form.

Type I. Explanation of a negative: multiple causes and a single/negative effect

Well over half of all applied social research is carried out in this inquiry structure. We have journals full of articles that try to explain delinquency, or mental illness, or low birth weight, or poverty, or some other problematic condition. This structure of inquiry focuses on problems via the lens of complex causality. This is the typical "multivariate" theory, though often it is a list of independent variables rather than a logically constructed theory. In its best form, a problem is explained in such a way that it might possibly be solved, but this is not usually the case. For applied purposes, one of the main flaws in this inquiry structure, as indicated above, is that no single independent variable is likely to be robust enough to warrant investment of resources. Another flaw is that, contrary to the main assumption in this theoretical logic, whatever causes a problem might not be the best way to un-cause it. It is often impractical or ineffectual to try to fix past or intractable circumstances, and resources might be better spent on something else.

Type II. Impact of a negative: single/negative cause and multiple effects

This inquiry structure is "one bad thing leads to others." Sometimes I think of this as *very bad for people* theory and research, as in "dropping out of school is very bad for people" or "using drugs is very bad for people" or "unemployment is very bad for people" and so on. In its best form, this inquiry structure can help document the extraordinarily high price that is paid for certain social problems. Some of the most striking examples are racial prejudice, sexual abuse, physical violence, undernourishment, illiteracy, and unemployment. A focus on multiple negative outcomes has been discussed in several areas of study, e.g., Cassel (1976), who examines the effects of stress on disease and points out that stress makes individuals vulnerable not to a specific stress-related disease, but to a wide array of diseases. If a health researcher assesses the effects of stress on a particular disease, the results may appear small or even insignificant, but this may miss other, perhaps multiple, effects of the stress that are very important to overall health status (Aneshensal et al., 1991). The implication of these studies is that the problem should be resolved, although this inquiry structure does not provide guidance on how to do that.

Type III. Explanation of a positive: multiple causes and a single/positive effect

Usually, the explanation of a positive is theoretically complex, e.g., many factors may contribute to higher income, including parent's status, family structure, psychological characteristics of the individual, and so on. As in Type I above, implications for action can be quite limited because so many factors are identified as contributing to the outcome of interest. Nonetheless, for applied purposes, this inquiry form may often be preferable to Type I because direct theoretical statements can be made about how people, families, groups, communities, and societies might do better, which may have immediate applied implications. Also, cumulative research might provide the building blocks that lead to explanation of a positive that has multiple effects (as in Type IV below), and in the long term this may be a productive strategy. For example, in other work we attend to multiple variables that might lead to savings and asset accumulation (Beverly and Sherraden, 1999), because it is likely that asset holding has multiple positive effects (Page-Adams and Sherraden, 1996).

Type IV. Impact of a positive: single/positive cause and multiple effects

This inquiry structure can be described as "one good thing leads to others." It is a structure that explicitly looks for "more bang for the buck," i.e., variance explained in more constructs that matter.[17] As indicated above, I believe that this is the best structure for intervention research and should be the backbone of the applied social sciences because it has the potential to identify what I call "strong independent variables" which, when transformed into application, can become "strong policies."[18] As a caveat, it may be that only a few independent constructs can be supported in this inquiry structure, and this

---

[17] I do not mean to imply here that explained variance on different dependent variables can in fact be numerically added up.

[18] The emphasis here is on general inquiry form for applied purposes. It is a 'big picture" view that does not address the theoretical specification that would be required for each of the multiple outcomes. Quite likely each hypothesized impact would have a different theory with mechanisms specified. This would require a multifaceted theory and research agenda. On the other hand, Vicente Espinoza raises the possibility and concern that the theory might not be specified in advance:

> You made clear that a strong policy is not an explanation, OK. It's neither a model of intervention as planners define it. I would compare your definition of strong policy to the start of a billiard game: the white ball would be your strong policy and the 15 colored balls in the triangle the system where you apply the policy. Billiards is an interesting game at the beginning because you never know-how the balls will scatter on the table. Although you can control the direction, strength, and rotation of the white ball, the outcome will always be different. In my understanding, the results cannot be defined as an "impact." One can only make general assumptions about the consequences the white ball might have on the system, like yours that positive outcomes will be larger than negative. This looks to me like an *ex-post* definition, which is rather risky in social planning. Lacking an adequate definition of goals, we are equally likely to identify strong policies and gross mistakes only after policies have been implemented.

This is a clear and very useful analogy, and I share this concern. In applied social science, theoretical statements should be specified in advance. This paper is that it is at the more abstract level of inquiry structure, however I do not mean to suggest that specific theory is not required.

is perhaps why it is infrequently used in the applied social sciences. Some examples of single/positive causes that have multiple effects (usually positive) might be: early childhood education, two-parent families, employment, and asset accumulation. In less developed countries, one can point to public sanitation, clear property rights, and education of girls.[19] If indeed there are only a small number of such constructs, a primary mission of the applied social sciences should be to identify and focus on them.

Applications to Youth Service

What is youth service?

It will be important to define youth service as an idea. Before we can get very far in building a knowledge base for youth service we will have to say what it is and what it is not. A definition might be *a period of service to community, society, or world, institutionalized as part of an opportunity structure for young people, with no or minimal financial compensation, but recognized and honored by society and the state.* But does this meet the test of a clear idea? Can most people easily understand it? At present, there is a great deal of work to do in stating and communicating youth service as an idea. The term can mean anything from informal voluntary activity to a centralized national service; military service is sometimes included; and youth service by youth is sometimes confused with social services provided *to* youth. A major

---

[19] Espinoza is skeptical about "one fits all" explanations, warning that in trying to explain too much, one can end up explaining nothing at all. His reasoning again relates to theoretical specificity, which he calls identifying the channels. Again, I agree with this point, but I do not agree that multiple explanations from a single construct do not exist. Indeed, it seems apparent that they do exist, probably in abundance. However, only a small number are likely to be overwhelmingly positive, and the challenge of public policy is to find these.

challenge for this field is to articulate a simple and coherent public image of youth service that is readily communicable.

Similarly, regarding specification for inquiry, youth service is not a single experience, but rather a bundle of experiences, including becoming part of a new organization, mentoring or supervision, responsibility for tasks, working with others, skill development, and so on. This may be a problem for research – how are we to know which aspect(s) of youth service have the most important impacts? But in fact youth service is probably no larger a bundle than other institutionalized roles such as education, marriage, employment, or membership in any organization. These constructs are often and usefully treated as integrated wholes for research purposes. Similarly, I suspect that a key to development of knowledge regarding youth service will be to achieve widespread institutional structures that define and promote it. If and when this is the case, service can be treated as a single construct in research the same way education is often treated as a single construct. Of course, there will always be important research questions that relate to aspects of youth service, but knowledge for policy purposes is unlikely to advance far until youth service is understood as an integrated whole.[20]

What are the multiple effects of youth service?

As indicated above, theory to guide research on youth service will ideally be constructed in the form of what is

---

[20] Both scholars and practitioners in youth service have raised important questions regarding context of youth service, especially the characteristics of the community and nation-state in which service occurs. In this regard, "service as an integrated whole" may be technically the same in two different places but very different in meaning and impact due to the nature of the community and/or the state. In this paper, I handle context as potential impacts of youth service, i.e., outcomes in social development and for the political state. This provides one kind of contextual information, but it is not the whole story.

labeled above the "impact of a positive." Along these lines, Donald Eberly has pointed out the multi-dimensional potential impacts of youth service:

> A sociologist views national service as a rite of passage from adolescence to adulthood. A patriot sees it as a training ground for building good citizens and national unity. An anti-poverty worker considers national service primarily as a service delivery program to the poor and needy. A manpower expert looks at national service as a way to facilitate the transition of young people from school to work. An inner-city resident hopes national service will reduce the incidence of neighborhood crime, poverty, drug abuse and unemployment. An educator believes national service will provide the experiential education needed to counter balance the years of largely passive education received by students in the classroom. An employer welcomes national service as an initiative that will yield good work habits, thereby reducing the risk of hiring young employees. A conservationist views national service as a source of labor that can restore the forests and wilderness areas to their condition of a century ago (Eberly, 1986).

Fortunately, we have a few examples of research that begin to identify multiple impacts. A study of state and local youth corps in the United States finds positive impacts on employment, earnings, personal and social responsibility, voting, and education, with larger impacts on African-American young men (Abt Associates, 1996). Another study finds that pregnancy is less likely for girls in community service, and school success is greater for both boys and girls. Looking at a randomly-assigned 283 girls who took part in the national Teen Outreach Program, mostly community service, throughout high school, researchers report a pregnancy rate of 4.2 percent, compared to a rate of 9.8 percent for 287 girls who took regular health and sex-education classes, but did not perform community service. The study also found that 27 percent of the Teen Outreach group, both girls and boys, failed courses during the five year study period, compared to 47 percent of the control group (Allen et al., 1997).

In a rudimentary application of this general approach, we have compared systems of non-military service in nine countries across eleven outcomes in five categories (Sherraden, Sherraden, and Eberly, 1990). The findings in this study are that "the commonweal" and "productivity" rank highest; "peace" and "state interests" rank lowest; and "benefits to participants" rank in the middle. These findings are based on simple ordinal ratings of outcomes of the programs, derived from documentary information and fieldwork in each of the countries. I summarize these categories because they emerged from prior research and field work and therefore may be a good starting place for thinking about multiple outcomes of youth service.[21]

Table 1. Outcomes of Youth Service in Nine Nations, 1990

Outcomes of Youth Service
 Ratings of Outcomes

The Commonweal
   Highest (3.5)
   Cultural Integration
   Citizenship
Productivity
   High (3.3)
   Social Development

---

[21] This section summarizes and extends Sherraden, Sherraden, and Eberly (1990).

Economic Development
Benefits to Participants
    Medium (2.2)
    Personal Development
    Education and Training
    Employment Opportunities
State Interests
    Low (1.9)
    Incorporation and Control
    Support for the Military
Peace
    Lowest (1.4)
    Conflict reduction ("Moral equivalent of war")
    International understanding

Source: Summarized from Sherraden, Sherraden, and Eberly (1990).

Notes: The nine countries are Canada, China, Costa Rica, Indonesia, Israel, Mexico, Nigeria, United States, and West Germany. The categories of outcomes emerged from the fieldwork. Ratings for categories are means across all nine countries, based on an ordinal scale ranging from one to five.

    <u>The commonweal</u>. In the 1990 study, commonweal outcomes of youth service was the highest ranked category overall. The commonweal refers to the public good, the general welfare, and the needs of the community as opposed to those of the individual. As Tocqueville observed long ago, in an individualistic, democratic nation, the ability of the society to work together is essential: "In democratic countries knowledge of how to combine is the mother of all other forms of knowledge; on its progress depends that of all others" (Tocqueville, 1969, p. 517). This thinking stands somewhat in contrast to the dominant individualistic form of liberal democracy in the United States, but it represents a strong undercurrent in America, exemplified by the work of John Dewey who observed, "The public has no hands except those of individual human beings" (1927, p. 82). More recently in this tradition,

Benjamin Barber (1984) has emphasized a community-oriented democracy. In sociological theory, commonweal issues are addressed under several headings, but historically one of the most prominent has been "social control." Social control in its classical meaning refers to attempts by society to self-regulate though social institutions and processes. It is explicitly oriented toward problem solving, expressed in concerns with community, commitment, citizenship, cooperation among diverse groups, and conflict resolution (Park and Burgess, 1921; Janowitz, 1975; Turner, 1976). Today the term social control has fallen into misuse, often understood in a negative sense as state control. The corruption of this term is unfortunate because no equally useful term has yet replaced it.

Another promising idea is social capital, which has recently become prominent (Coleman, 1990; Putnam, 1993, 1995, 2000).[22] At this stage of its development, social capital is a somewhat amorphous concept. As it is refined and perhaps specified into several forms, social capital may have the potential to guide intellectual and applied advancements related to youth service. What is needed is the identification of constructs that represent social capital, or various aspects of social capital, and development of measures for these constructs that might be used to assess impacts of youth service or other Type IV interventions.

Cultural integration and political tolerance. Margaret Mead (1967) observed that "the poor and rich, the highly technologically gifted and those with obsolescent skills, the white collar and the blue collar, are each reared in almost total ignorance of one another." Mead suggested that a universal

---

[22] Putnam undertook the empirical research in Italy that led to today's prominence of social capital in sociology, political science, public policy, and community development. It is rare that a single study launches a concept into such prominence, with wide-ranging debate and inquiry, in this case both academic and applied.

national service would compensate for the increasing "fragmentation, ignorance, and lack of knowledge of their fellow citizens." For example, youth service in programs such as the National Youth Service of Nigeria (Enemuo, 2000) and Katimavik in Canada (Ninacs and Toye, 2000) have adopted cultural integration and political tolerance as the primary theme.

Citizenship. One of the most prominent viewpoints in discussions of youth service is the sociology of citizenship, represented by the work of T.H. Marshall (1950, 1977) and Morris Janowitz (1980, 1983). Essentially, this perspective focuses on the evolution and balance of citizenship rights vs. obligations, and on institutional structures that facilitate or impede expression of citizenship responsibilities. From this viewpoint, a program of youth service facilitates individual contributions to the nation and the building of national bonds (Etzioni, 1983; Sherraden and Eberly, 1984; Moskos, 1988). Moskos, for example, rejects the artificial split between "tough minded" military service and "high minded" civilian service. Both, he suggests, should be tied together with the theme of civic commitment. In practice, many variations of the citizenship theme exist. In some nations, citizenship is embodied in mandatory service obligations, while in other nations it is entirely voluntary but supported by social institutions. Using youth service as an expression of citizenship may provide a new basis for policy-making in the youth sector (Espinoza, 2000).

Productivity. Also ranked high in terms of impacts of youth service in our 1990 study was productivity, or the value of the service projects given the input. Somewhat arbitrarily, this discussion occurs under two headings -- social development and economic development.

Social development. The concept of social development was first used in the context of developing nations to call attention to the human/social side of development.[23] Originally it was a reaction to rigid economic thinking about development (Ul Haq and Streeten, 1995). The initial emphasis was on basic living conditions and social protections, but in recent years it has become more and more clear that the greatest economic resource in any nation is its people, as both human capital and social capital. With this realization, interest in social development has grown. A United Nations sponsored world summit for social development was held in 1995 and this term is now in greater use and has spread to advanced economies (e.g., Midgley, 1995). Youth service is often seen as a tool for solving social problems and promoting social development. The emphasis is on assisting particular individuals and groups -- such as the illiterate, the disabled, the elderly, and children -- primarily through activities that could be broadly classified as human services (Eberly, 1970). Yarmolinsky (1977) and Danzig and Szanton (1986) take this perspective on non-military service almost exclusively. In general, these studies show large unmet human needs that are not likely to be addressed in the private marketplace, and therefore some type of institutionalized service may have a positive impact on social development.

Economic development. A related perspective views youth service as a mechanism for economic development. Emphasis on economic development typically concentrates on use of available resources, in this case youth labor, and the value of the service product. In the United States, the historical example of the Civilian Conservation Corps stands out as being enormously productive in tree planting and building of state and national park facilities (Salmond, 1967; Sherraden, 1979). The viewpoint of economic productivity is often taken explicitly in developing countries, where more than half of the

---

[23] Social development and social capital have something in common. It may be useful to think of social capital as relational capacities, and social development as actions using those capacities as resources.

population can be under 18 years of age. As we enter the twenty-first century, 80 to 85 percent of the youth population lives in the developing world, much of it in the informal labor market. In the year 2010 the population of the world will reach 6.8 billion, with 1.7 billion young people between the ages of 15 and 24, and 86 percent of these in developing counties. In most developing nations, a large portion of the youth population is either unemployed or employed in the informal labor market (Ruiz, 2000). The economic development perspective on youth service views the large youth population as an underutilized resource. Ruiz (2000) takes this a step further and suggests that youth service can be the foundation of a new "economics of solidarity" in which the economy serves the people, rather than the other way around, and "people interact to formulate solutions other than those offered by either the market or the state." Major issues in the economic development impacts of youth service include the degree to which young people working on a short-term basis can actually be productive, the danger of exploiting young people in this process, bridges from service to formal labor markets, and the potential to disrupt employment of adults.

Benefits to participants. In our 1990 study we found benefits to participants to rank as medium in terms of outcomes of youth service. In this sense, programs of youth service are policy instruments in the tradition of the modern welfare state, wherein the state takes responsibility for assisting individual citizens. Less developed nations have systems of state-provided services as well, though typically less encompassing. In different countries, benefits to individuals may different forms in the areas of education, housing, health care, food, employment, disability protection, family supports, and retirement security. The focus in this paper is not the entire array of social welfare services, but rather the extent to which programs of youth service are used to provide such benefits. For the sake of brevity, only three of the most important types of benefits of youth service are discussed here --

personal development, education and training, and employment opportunities.

   Personal development, connections to adulthood.   In addition to the moral equivalent of war, William James (1910) expressed a vision of personal development through service. He said that participants would have the "childishness knocked out of them."   Social scientists and policy makers have sometimes turned to youth service to counter negative trends among young people (e.g., Mead, 1967; Erikson, 1967). The focus is typically on psychological development and maturation. In this regard, proponents may speak of a system of youth service as a "rite of passage" for young people in moving from adolescence to adulthood. Mead suggested that a system of youth service might prevent some young people from going into early marriages "as a device to reach pseudo-adult status." She believed that service might provide an opportunity to establish an identity and sense of self-respect before making career choices or establishing homes, and she saw this as quite valuable, especially for many young women. Erikson suggested a period of "moratorium" from the relentless pressures of deciding on a career. James Coleman (1972) and his colleagues on the Panel on Youth of the President's Science Advisory Committee concluded that the transition to adulthood is impeded in modern industrial society, and dependency is prolonged. According to Coleman, modern youth are "education rich" but "action poor," the reverse of the situation a century earlier. Under these circumstances, a youth culture has taken shape that is inward looking, consumption-oriented, and largely segregated from adult responsibilities and values. As a response to this situation, Coleman recommended deliberate creation of new institutions for public service.

   Education and training.   Another developmental perspective is education and training. In this case, service is viewed as an opportunity for learning, work experience, or career exploration, and is defined as study-service, service learning, or learning through practice. Youth service along these dimensions has been proposed by Coleman (1972), the Carnegie Commission on Higher Education (1973), Wirtz (1975), and White (1978). During the 1980s and 1990s service learning has been in the ascendancy in the United States. A growing number of secondary schools and universities require and/or actively promote community service, which is often accompanied by a structured service learning component. For example, Campus Compact was created in 1985 to promote service by university students in the United States and today has 570 member institutions and 20 state compacts, promoting service learning requirements. As a result, service learning is growing as an accepted component of higher education (Jacoby et al., 1996).

Employment opportunities. Unemployment as an issue for young people is not only a cyclical problem, but a long-term historical trend. The trend in industrial economies has been for young people to be pushed out of the labor market (Osterman, 1980; Sherraden, 1987, 1991b). It may be that, with the advent of the information age, this trend will reverse because young people may adapt to information technology and the "new economy" more readily than adults (Krauskopf, 2000). In some nations, goals of youth service focus on employment of the youth population, and indeed, youth employment has been a major consideration in youth service proposals in the United States. A prominent issue in these policies is whether the work genuinely needs to be done. In the United States, some youth employment policies, for example, the Summer Youth Employment Program, have been little more than a make-work, keep-them-off-the-streets programs (Sherraden, 1980; Sherraden and Adamek, 1984). On the other hand, many youth service programs may not emphasize employment but still have positive impacts on work experience, skill development, and exploration of different career paths.

State interests. National programs of youth service may serve at least some interests of the political state, though we did not find this to be a common impact of youth service in our 1990 study. State interests do not have to be detrimental to society, but they sometimes are. To some pro-market, anti-government critics, organized service is viewed as a misuse of state power. For example, Milton Friedman (1979) once called organized non-military service a "monstrosity utterly inconsistent with a free society." A similar orientation is sometimes voiced on the progressive Left. There is reason for this concern. The Hitler Youth of Nazi Germany and the Red Guard of the Cultural Revolution period in China cannot be forgotten as youth "service" organizations that were turned to evil purposes of the state. These horrific historical examples should not be downplayed or dismissed, but they do not represent the vast majority of youth service policies and programs around the globe.

Incorporation and control. An important viewpoint in understanding youth service is as centralized control, often discussed in terms of incorporation or corporatist state theory, which focuses on the role of state policy in integrating, sometimes co-opting, individuals and groups into the state political apparatus. From this point of view, youth service (in this case national service) would be seen as a mechanism to enhance loyalty of individuals and interest groups to the state, and accordingly, might serve narrow interests of the political elite. A great deal of policy research, particularly in developing nations, has concluded that policy may be guided by efforts of the federal government to link population groups to the state (Stepan, 1978; Schmitter and Lehmbruch, 1980). This occurs to some extent in youth service, sometimes under the banner of "cultural integration" (reaching out and incorporating marginal population groups), but we have not found it to be a prominent theme.

Support for the military. Proposals for non-military national service almost inevitably lead to a discussion of one particular state interest -- support of the military. In the United States, a frequent reaction from the progressive left to proposals for non-military service is that such proposals are, or might be, covers for a return to a military draft. In nations where there is a respected non-military service option, e.g., Germany, the non-military service option in an important sense legitimizes the military and makes it acceptable. Also, in those countries where the military itself actually performs significant non-military activities, these activities may be used by the state to gain support for the military. Thus, there are a number of ways in which the political state can use youth service, particularly national service, to gain support for the military. However, we have not found this to be a common theme. For example, AmeriCorps in the United States has virtually no interaction or influence on military service.[24]

Peace. Peace, defined as reduction of international conflict or promotion of international understanding, was found to be a very minor impact of youth service in our 1990 study. There are relatively few examples of cross-border, international elements of youth service.

Conflict reduction. William James's (1910) essay, "The Moral Equivalent of War," provides a starting point in many discussions of non-military youth service in the United States. James believed that militarism had to be re-channeled. In the interests of international peace, he proposed an institutional equivalent of war, in his words, "an army against Nature." His proposal was based on a psychodynamic perspective of innate aggression as a part of human nature. But does an individual, psychological view make sense at the level of social institutions? In this regard, can non-military service

---

[24] If AmeriCorps were significantly larger, it would likely have an impact on military recruitment.

re-channel innate aggression, and replace war, in the sense that William James suggested? It is possible to conceive of an institutional restructuring of militarism -- nations might send "armies of peace" as a moral equivalent of war. Conflict might be resolved according to who could build the best highway, dam, or oil pipeline in the opposing nation, rather than who could destroy the same, but this is a long way from reality. At one time, there was a small and hopeful body of scholarship under the heading of "peaceful uses of military forces" (Glick, 1967; Hanning, 1967), and there are modern examples of armies used for civilian purposes, but as appealing as this swords-into-plowshares theme might sound at first glance, it is in fact risky and problematic. The risk is that non-military functions and operations will become militarized, rather than the other way around.

International understanding. Youth service might promote peace in other ways, and one prominent theme is international understanding. From this perspective, youth service would be international service, designed to improve mutual understanding and appreciation, promote tolerance, and develop interpersonal and inter-institutional bonds. One of the books most associated with this viewpoint is Eugen Rosenstock-Huessy's *Planetary Service* (1978). Rosenstock-Huessy's vision is a supra-national service. In his view, peace is not absence of war, but rather active involvement and participation across borders. This is likely to be a much more fruitful approach to the theme of peace in youth service. A current example is the plan for a cross-border Arab-Israeli service as outlined in Gal's (2000) paper on youth service in Israel. Recently, the North American Institute at Stanford and the Ford Foundation sponsored a symposium on the possibility of youth service in North America, and issues regarding integration of youth service in the three nations of Canada, the United States, and Mexico were presented (Sherraden and Sherraden, 1999).

As a summary thought, William James's essay on the moral equivalent of war has served important political and public awareness purposes, but as a way of understanding the impacts of youth service in our time, it is of limited value. The outcomes of youth service are far more diverse and complex, and the greatest outcomes are in areas of the commonweal, productivity, and benefits to participants.

Directions for Research and Policy

Worldwide, there is a large body of experience regarding youth service and a great deal has been learned. For example, in the United States, we have a policy legacy that suggests strongly that we know how to undertake a youth service policy. Eberly (1986) has pointed to four major lessons from previous or existing US programs. The Civilian Conservation Corps (CCC) taught us that the government could organize and manage a large, residential, and effective youth service program. The GI Bill for Education revealed the value of a service in providing a foundation for further education among all classes of young people. The Peace Corps has demonstrated that young people can be trusted to do important international work other than in the Armed Forces. VISTA (Volunteers in Service to America) has demonstrated that young people can serve effectively at home as well as overseas, and that even impoverished young people are willing to serve as volunteers on subsistence stipends.

To these we might add important lessons from many other programs, such as the National Youth Administration of the 1930s, Job Corps from the 1960s to the present, numerous state and local conservation and service corps since the 1980s, and AmeriCorps, the US youth service that was created in 1993. In addition to this practical experience, the United States has always had a bipartisan and political consensus in general support of youth service programs. The CCC was among the most popular of New Deal programs; VISTA and the Peace Corps have been supported by the Congress, even when the White House has been opposed. AmeriCorps has been politically troubled not so much because politicians are against the concept, but because AmeriCorps was President Clinton's signature program during a very partisan political period. Overall, the practical challenges to large-scale youth service do not appear to be formidable. Many of us have long had the sense that it could happen in the United States, if things were to fall into place.[25] But things have not fallen into place, and it is incumbent on us to ask why.

Knowledge building

In my view, we do not know enough. Both the concept of service and its impacts are unclear. We have not yet built a sufficient base of theory and empirical research to support youth service, and in the absence of a strong knowledge base we cannot sustain the idea in the political process. Advocates of youth service have operated mostly in the realm of well-intentioned value statements and beliefs, with historical and anecdotal examples, but without a convincing way to understand youth service and support it with empirical evidence. The field of youth service is in need of stronger and multi-faceted theory that can capture the public's imagination, serve as a framework for collecting and understanding empirical evidence, and guide policy innovation. As indicated in this paper, I believe that the structure of inquiry to guide research should be to look for "impact of a positive" (Type IV above). In this formulation, youth service would be tested as a "strong independent variable" that is likely to have multiple positive impacts. In the policy arena, application could be thought of as "strong policy" because impacts would be multiple and returns on public investment would potentially be

---

[25] In this section I have used US examples because I know them better than others, though I would guess that this level of experience and practical "know how" with youth exists in many other countries, and much more in some.

high. To move in this direction, a number of conceptual and analytical tools can be brought to bear. Below I point to three tools that "fit" the Type IV inquiry structure and may be promising.

Theoretical approach: neo-functionalism or something like it. Functionalism is a major sociological tradition, with roots in the work of Compte, Spencer, and Durkheim. In modern sociology, functionalism was revived by Parsons (1951) and others. The essence of functional analysis is that social structures have their particular characteristics because they serve particular functions in society. In essence, function determines structure. Therefore, the search is for functional requisites of particular social structures. During the 1960s, functionalism was much debated and criticized, and remains controversial. The central criticisms of functionalist theory have been that it is essentially conservative because it is ahistorical and provides an implicit rationale for the status quo, and it does not incorporate conflict perspectives. However, these shortcomings are probably not inherent features of functional analysis, but rather may have more to do with the subject matter of the early functionalist theorists. The recognition that critiques of functionalism may not be well founded has led to somewhat of a revival of functional theory among neo-functionalists (Alexander, 1985).

A neo-functional approach has particular value during early phases of inquiry in the categorization of social systems, which is where the study of youth service is at present. Turner and Maryanski (1988) observe that much neo-functionalist analysis is macro, comparative, and essentially taxonomic, and it is through this usage that neo-functionalism is making its greatest contribution. The goal of neo-functional study of youth service would be to identify, categorize, and give relative weight to the various functions (or outcomes) of service. The tapestry of functions and outcomes that emerges within countries and across countries may yield a rich and complex, yet patterned and meaningful interpretation. This is how neo-functionalism, or some similar approach, can make a contribution in studies of youth service. Within this framework, multiple research methods, from case studies to large-scaled comparative surveys, can contribute to knowledge building.[26]

Statistical analysis: simultaneous explanation. In the past, a severe limitation on studying multiple dependent variables has been the lack of technical ability to estimate multiple equations simultaneously. But with increasing statistical power, these limitations are eased. Structural equation modeling (SEM) is one example of an analytical tool that can handle multiple dependent variables in simultaneous statistical tests (Bollen, 1989; Joreskog and Sorbom, 1993). As such, it is well suited to the Type IV inquiry structure described above. To illustrate, we have used SEM to test another type of "strong policy" – asset building (mentioned above). Using the Panel Study of Income Dynamics (PSID), a large, longitudinal data set, we were able to test a number of these hypothesized effects, and at the same time test two main alternative explanations (Yadama and Sherraden, 1996). The ability to ask all of these questions simultaneously of the same set of longitudinal data is nearly as close to causal explanation as the social sciences can reach at present. The potential for such tools in studies of youth service and its impacts is great. But in order to reach this potential, youth service will have to be included in future survey waves of PSID and other on-going social research data sets. Looking ahead, the creation and incorporation of youth service measures in major survey instruments should be a high priority of scholars in this field.

Policy tool: benefit-cost analysis. Benefit-cost analysis (BCA) and its cousin, cost effectiveness analysis (CEA), are of course well-established techniques for policy analysis.

---

[26] This comment builds on a footnote in Sherraden, Sherraden, and Eberly (1990).

BCA asks about the ratio of benefits to costs in dollar value, while CEA asks about the cost to achieve a given impact that is not measured in dollars. In more complex applications, impacts in CEA are multiple and combined in an index. BCA is implicitly comparative because of the universal dollar measure. CEA is meaningful only when two or more alternative programs or policies are being compared. BCA and CEA tend to wax and wane in popularity, but they have bedrock qualities that are likely to keep them around as basic policy analysis tools (Brent, 1996) in both developed and developing nations (e.g., Schreiner, 1999). BCA is particularly well suited to Type IV inquiry structure because it asks explicitly about different types of benefits (multiple impacts) on different groups (e.g., individuals, organizations, society). In this regard, BCA has much in common with neo-functionalism and structural equation modeling because it can handle multiple impacts of a single construct or intervention. BCA is the policy analysis tool of choice for studying "strong policy." Fortunately, there have been several applications of BCA in youth service evaluations, and results are usually positive. For example, a study of the Conservation and Youth Service Corps in the United States reports a net benefit of $1.04 per hour (Abt Associates, 1996). The major challenge in using BCA in any context is that there is never a single "right" answer; a great deal depends on what is included as costs and benefits. This again points to the importance of theory. With sound theoretical specification, it is easier to identify benefits to be measured, and to defend research results. Where BCA is not possible due to inability to monetize benefits, CEA can be usefully applied to compare two or more forms of youth service, or youth service vs. an alternative youth policy or policies, in terms of how efficiently they generate desirable impacts.

Policy Development

In this paper I have suggested that weakness in theory and empirical evidence is the major barrier to youth service policy development, but it is not the only barrier. Many factors will have to work in concert to move policy forward.

Vision. Not least of these is the articulation of a large and compelling vision of why youth service (or service across the life span) should be a new social institution that engages many people in the affairs of community and society, and recognizes these contributions. In the past, I have suggested that the historical retreat of the industrial labor market from young people makes a new social institution for the transition to adulthood a compelling need (Sherraden, 1991b). However, with the transition to the information age, this may not be as strong an argument in the future as it has been in the past. In the information economy and society, young people may engage in adult-like roles at much earlier ages (Krauskopf, 2000).

Another candidate for a vision for service is to turn to the opposite end of the age spectrum, where discussions of useful roles for older adults and "productive aging" is increasing (Morrow-Howell et al., forthcoming). With aging populations in most countries, it is possible that large new social institutions for service will first occur with seniors as the major constituency. Danzig and Szanton (1986) foresaw this possibility and suggested that service by older adults might develop more rapidly than service by youths. Emerging discussions of productive aging are an opening to promote service across the life span, with service opportunities available at all ages.

Another possible vision is service as a counter balance to the increasing dominance of capitalism and self-interest around the globe. For this vision to be convincing, it will have to be shown that people are indeed in retreat from community and social responsibility (Putnam, 1995), and that there is an unacceptable cost for this retreat because large positive impacts can result from social involvement (Woolcock, 1998). Many people in fact believe this, but this vision has not been adequately articulated. This may be a particular challenge in the United States because it runs counter to individualistic values, which are dominant.[27]

Whatever the substantive vision, the Type IV inquiry structure would seem to be promising in shaping and supporting the vision by asking about multiple positive impacts. If these can be articulated as part of the vision, and later specified and tested empirically, the vision is more likely to capture the public's imagination and garner support in the policy process.

Engagement. Sociologists tend to talk about new policies and institutions as being created by "social forces" converging in a particular way at a particular time, and there is some truth to these types of explanations. But the other part of the truth is that new policies and institutions are conceived, enacted, implemented, and nurtured by creativity, capability, and commitment, usually by a small number of key individuals and organizations. In this sense, policies and institutions are not created by abstract social forces, but are *made to happen* by real people. For example, in youth service in the United States, Franklin D. Roosevelt held the vision for the CCC; Hubert Humphrey kept the idea alive in the Congress; Donald Eberly and his National Service Secretariat led policy formation in Washington over several decades; Morris Janowitz provided intellectual leadership that is not yet fully

---

[27] Many people have pointed out that not all impacts of social capital are likely to be positive (e.g., Woolcock, 1998; Durlauf, 1999). To be sure, this would be true of any concept or policy, including youth service. The challenge is to identify key concepts and strong policies whose impacts are mostly, perhaps even overwhelmingly, positive. The fact that some negative impacts are possible should not deter a search for strong policies. At the end of the day, the weight of evidence, not single contrary examples, should be the determining factor.

recognized; Franklin Thomas of the Ford Foundation provided foundation vision and support; Howard Swearer and Susan Stroud initiated Campus Compact; Charles Moskos shaped the policy concept and the Democratic Leadership Council initiated the policy process that led to AmeriCorps;[28] Harris

---

[28] Susan Stroud, who was working in the White House during the passage of AmeriCorps, reminds me that the political process is a lot more complex and multi-faceted than this brief summary suggests, and many different political interests in fact shape the resulting policy so that it is not clear and simple, but multi-faceted. In Stroud's words:

> The group of us working in the White House in 1993 who put together AmeriCorps may have lacked a clear theoretical basis for what we did, but we had sound ideas generally. However, regardless of how good and theoretically-grounded they may or may not have been, they were modified by (1) the President, who had his own ideas and sense of what would sell politically, (2) presidential advisors such as Gene Sperling and the Democratic Leadership Council who were attempting to fit the program into the larger Clinton agenda, hence the emphasis on "reinventing government" in the design of the Corporation. . . , (3) other administration officials, e.g., the team of Education Secretary Riley, (4) various constituencies, e.g., we couldn't combine VISTA totally with AmeriCorps, and we kept the Points of Light Foundation, which Clinton Promised Bush he wouldn't eliminate, (5) members of Congress, e.g., we had to satisfy Sonny Montgomery regarding the size of AmeriCorps benefits vs. veterans benefits, and on and on. The resulting policy is a case study of sausage making, and a useful metaphor for AmeriCorps is a Swiss Army knife that has multiple functions (see Steve Waldman's book), rather like your "strong policy" idea (Stroud email to Sherraden, December 5, 1999, text altered slightly for clarity).

These comments remind us that many people work very hard and make numerous compromises before a concept is enacted as a major public policy. An important insight in these comments is that the policy process itself may yield (perhaps typically yields) a policy that is multi-faceted and *because of this* likely to have multiple impacts. This is quite a different view of how a "strong policy" might come about. In this paper, I have attempted to argue from a neat and tidy rational perspective – first the idea,

Wofford, former director of AmeriCorps, has in recent years played a crucial role in working successfully with a very partisan Congress; and there are many others. Each country will have its individual and organizational exemplars of engagement for youth service.

However, the capacity to engage in this field, both in the United States and around the world, today seems inadequate. Youth service initiatives, following a period of development in the 1980s and early 1990s, in recent years appear to have settled on a plateau. To move to the next level, leadership and engagement will be required. Especially given increasing globalization, there is a need for capacity building that can support policy and program development around the world. Strategies for this increased capacity include not only specifying theory and doing more and better research, but also providing guidance and tools for research, creating a web-based information network, publishing key studies and reports, strengthening international ties and organizations, and supporting international meetings so that lessons can be transferred among countries.

Summary and Conclusion

In summation, I would return to some basic observations about inquiry in the applied social sciences that have implications for youth service research and policy. First, there is a severe gap in knowledge about youth service. This includes a fuzziness of the concept, lack of theoretical specificity, and insufficient empirical evidence of impacts.

---

then the application, and then the evidence. Stroud's brief example of AmeriCorps documents that the democratic process, messy and irrational as it is, may in fact be a generator of strong policy, but in unpredictable ways. As with most apparent opposites, this is not really an either/or choice. Both perspectives are important and necessary. If we are aiming to enact a strong policy, clear ideas and theory are a good beginning, and engaging in the policy process is always required.

Second, I have argued that selection of inquiry structure may be the foremost issue, often more important than other decisions of theory and research that follow. Third, the inquiry form that I have called "impact of a positive" (Type IV) is likely to be a productive structure for the applied social sciences because it has the potential to point to a "strong policy." Youth service may be among a perhaps small and select class of concepts that are ideally suited for public policy because impacts are likely to be multiple and positive. To date we have not harnessed this perspective to generate a body of evidence to support youth service. In the future this thinking may lead to more carefully specified theory and documentation of a full range of impacts of youth service. The weight of such evidence, when purposefully engaged in the policy process, would have the potential to tip the scale of policy formation.

$$* \qquad * \qquad * \qquad * \qquad *$$

As a closing thought, I would like to step back and offer a long-term observation. It seems likely that civic service is a slowly emerging social institution that one day could be as common and accepted as, for example, employment and education are today. During a lengthy institutional birthing process, when civic service sometimes seems like a fuzzy and poorly understood concept, and when the knowledge base is weak, it may be helpful to keep a historical perspective in mind. Labor markets and employment were at one time a fuzzy and disruptive innovation. Widespread public education, which we take for granted today, was in the late 19th century a fuzzy and controversial innovation. Those who are advocates of civic service should understand the nature of large-scale institutional change, and take some satisfaction in how far it has come already. In the latter half of the twentieth century, national non-military service programs have arisen and today number at least in the twenties. U.S. Presidents (Kennedy and Clinton) have made a particular point of calling for service. There are a wide range of civic service forms, and activity in many countries. Civic service is now being discussed not only for youth, but also for adults and elders, across the life span. Today, for the first time, there is a worldwide understanding that civil society and civic engagement are crucial for democratic governance. All of these developments suggest that civic service is emerging, in fits and starts, on a broad scale. Thoughtful inquiry in applied research can inform and enhance this policy development.

PART IV

THE FUTURE OF NATIONAL YOUTH SERVICE

In moving from large-scale military service to large-scale NYS, there are various ways in which NYS cadets can serve with soldiers and others involved in post-war and post-disaster reconstruction. There are also numerous techniques for accomplishing the gradual introduction of NYS. Finally, we take a brief look at what can be expected from substantial NYS programs and suggest a conceptual framework for NYS.

CHAPTER 9

A POTENTIAL ROLE FOR NYS IN COMMUNITY RECONSTRUCTION AND INTERCULTURAL UNDERSTANDING

War and the threat of war lead nations to increase their military budgets, to prepare its citizens to fight the perceived enemy, and to mobilize its young people to do battle with other young people on the front lines. Wars have consequences lasting far beyond the end of the battle. Young people in NYS can play a vital role in post-war community reconstruction, in maintaining peace in tense situations, and perhaps in preventing war. In many places torn apart by conflict and war, the civic muscles that hold together the fabric of society have not only been weakened but elements of civic society have been disrupted, if not destroyed.

In writing this chapter one of us (RG) relied both on the growing body of literature and research focusing on community and social-process typical of the post cold-war era, and on his personal experiences and professional observations in various troubled countries and regions for more than a decade. These areas include Northern Ireland, the former Soviet Union, the former Yugoslavia, Japan, and Nigeria.

Coming from my own turbulent region in the Middle East, I have learned to identify and be attentive to the unique and particular characteristics of each conflict, while at the same time drawing general conclusions and seeing common denominators. This chapter focuses on those common denominators and conclusions.

The Nature of Wars and Their Aftermath

There is a congruence between the characteristics of certain wars and the characteristics of their aftermaths and recovery periods.

Total wars, between two or more states, or between coalitions of state-allies, end in whatever way they end, whether with a decisive victory by one side or with an ambiguous conclusion. In the sequel period each side licks its wounds and engages in its own post-war reconstruction.

Civil wars, on the other hand, or protracted conflicts between neighboring entities, last a long time, do not end with a clear 'winner' or 'loser,' and typically reach their end because of both-sides' exhaustion, a dead-end situation, external intervention, or some combination thereof. A civil war often involves countless communities where neighbors suddenly find themselves at war with each other. It is not just a war, but a war between those who were once friends and colleagues. Social norms of civic-minded behavior, which may have existed previously, can be decimated by distrust and conflict.

When the fighting stops and efforts are focused on recovery, community rehabilitation is as critical as physical reconstruction or individual rehabilitation. The period of recuperation and rebuilding of the social fabric and mechanisms for civic engagement may prove to be the most challenging phase. While citizens may have watched helplessly as their country was torn apart by ethnic or religious conflict, they now must return to learning how to be neighbors, friends, and colleagues once again. Communities must again create a sense of joint purpose, where networks of trust are developed and mechanisms exist for citizens to involve themselves in a collaborative process of problem solving.

Furthermore, while a total war is identified with the top leaders -- as was the case in World War II with Hitler,

Stalin, Churchill and Roosevelt -- centrally-organized military corps, fully obedient to a clear hierarchy of authority, conduct the war itself. And the entire population, across all its communities, feels strong identification with the "collective" homeland.

By contrast, in almost all civil wars, the leadership is not clearly distinct, the fighting is frequently conducted by different militia-groups varying in their ideological reasoning, and it is the local and communal identity that many times exceeds the collective identification. Again, the historical illustration could be seen at the turn of the 21st Century in the Middle East, among both Palestinians and Israelis. These characteristics of civil wars were also very apparent among the Catholics and Protestants in Northern Ireland, in the civil wars in Nigeria and South Africa, and also in the former Yugoslav states.

The cause of the war, then, determines the way the war is conducted which, in turn, is congruent with what happens after the war. It is not only *"la guerre comme la guerre,"* but also *"la post-guerre comme la guerre."*

And so, in the post-war era that follows a civil war or a protracted ethnic conflict, the internal processes at the communal, grass-roots, and civic level are as important as they were during the war – and much more so! Furthermore, it has been my observation that the more confident each of the adversary groups in a civil war becomes in terms of its own self-identity, the more tolerant toward the "other" it will grow, and subsequently, the closer and better will be the solution of the conflict. This was, indeed, the case in Northern Ireland and in South Africa; and this is what will happen inevitably in the Middle East and in Southeast Europe. In some respects, what happened in the former Yugoslav countries around the turn of the century reflects exactly that, albeit predominantly at the national, rather than the communal level. The election outcomes in Croatia, Serbia and to a certain extent also in Bosnia-Herzegovina showed that the people in these countries had been turning away from extreme nationalistic positions and into more tolerant and "internal" politics.

Similarly, this trend is reflected in local initiatives to promote regional conflict-resolution activities. One such initiative was made in 2001 by Prof. Dean Ajdukovic. The primary aim of Ajdukovic's proposal is "to develop constructive conflict management approaches in communities in order to facilitate the social reconstruction and rebuilding of civil society and consequently the recovery from turmoil." (SPA, 2001).

Modes of Recovery and Community Reconstruction

Mental-health professionals have been traditionally alerted to help affected civilians, predominately children, after (or during) mass-disaster situations to recover from the trauma and to prevent a long-term impairment, such as post-traumatic stress disorder. Normally this help is comprised of mental support, expressions of empathy, and the provision of legitimacy for experiencing post-distress difficulties. In more serious cases, the treatment is aimed at strengthening idiosyncratic coping mechanisms. Depending on the particular individual, these coping modes can fall into one or more of the following categories:

- ☐ Focusing on <u>affect/emotional processing</u> (enabling the abreaction of effect, transforming uncontrollable anxieties into tolerable fears, etc.);
- ☐ Focusing on <u>cognitive processing</u> (re-framing the situation, or manipulating the person's cognitive appraisal) ;
- ☐ Focusing on the <u>active-behavioral processing</u> (encouraging active behavior, practicing preferred behavioral patterns, etc.).

In areas undergoing severe trauma, whether following man-made evils such as wars, terrorist acts, and atrocities; or nature-made disasters such as earthquakes, hurricanes, and tsunamis, both local and international projects have been initiated to provide training and professional supervision for such psychological help. Typically, however, these psycho-social programs focused on traumatized individuals and shattered families. Rarely did they expand beyond the family realm and into the community, the larger society, or regional domains but when they did, these more holistic approaches have helped to heal societies in the aftermath of terrible crises. Affect-, cognitive-, and active-behavioral processing can and should be applied to whole communities, not only to individuals. This is where NYS programs, manned by young and typically healthy men and women, can become a major source of help, by strengthening the local community and its services.

Several key concepts have emerged in the last twenty years within the social sciences that reflect this shift of focus from the individual-based to the community-based modes of post-stress recovery. I would like to focus on three – Social Capital, Citizenship Behavior and Service-Learning – as leading examples in this evolving area.

Social Capital. Surfacing in the 1980's (and even before), the term social capital became widely used only in the last decade of the 20th Century, mostly through the fascinating field research conducted by Robert Putnam (1993) in support of this conceptualization. Social capital is defined as 'features of social organization, such as trust, norms, and networks, that can improve the efficiency of society by facilitating coordinated actions' (Putnam, 1993; p.167). James Coleman (note 3) describes it in more colloquial words: "The more extensively persons call on one another for aid, the greater will be the quantity of social capital generated.... Social relationships die out if not maintained: expectations and obligations wither over time; and norms depend on regular communication." (Coleman, 1990, p.321). It is Coleman also who provides *in-vivo* examples that illustrate how social capital can become a powerful, very basic, resource. Here are two examples:

☐ "A mother of six children, who moved with her husband and children from suburban Detroit to Jerusalem, describes as one reason for doing so the greater freedom her young children have in Jerusalem. She feels it is safe to let her eight-year-old take the six–year-old across town to school on the city bus and to let her children play without supervision in a city park, neither or which did she feel able to allow where she lived before. The reason for this difference can be described as a difference in the social capital available in Jerusalem and in suburban Detroit. In Jerusalem the normative structure ensures that unattended children will be looked after by adults in the vicinity, but no such normative structure exists in most metropolitan areas of the United States. One can say that families in Jerusalem have available to them social capital that does not exist in metropolitan areas of the United States." (p.303). (note 4)

☐ "In the central market in Cairo, the boundaries between merchants are difficult for an outsider to discover. The owner of a shop which specializes in leather, when queried about where one finds a certain kind of jewelry, will turn out to sell that as well – or what appears to be nearly the same thing, to have a close associate who sells it, to whom he will immediately take the customer. Or a shopkeeper will instantly become a money-changer simply by turning to his colleague a few shops down. For some activities, such as bringing a customer to a friend's store, there are commissions; others, such as money changing, merely create obligations. Family relations are important in the market, as is the stability of proprietorship. The whole market is so infused with relations of the sort just described that it can be seen as an organization, no less so than a department store. Alternatively, the market can be seen as consisting of a set of individual merchants, each having an extensive body of social capital on which to draw, based on the relationship within the market." (p.304)

Social capital, then, is enhanced by social norms, habits and tradition. But it is further developed and facilitated by simple communal activities such as citizens' meetings, neighborhood gatherings, social clubs (e.g. folk-dancing, music-listening, card-playing), voluntary team-work, and self-support groups.

One classic way of enhancing social capital is by applying voluntary youth service within the community, or within a given society across its diverse communities. Following William James' famous call for a "moral equivalent of war" (James, 1910), today there are numerous frameworks around the world of youth volunteers serving within their communities in civic roles covering health, welfare, education, environment and many more areas. Of particular interest are those frameworks operating in big (and troublesome!) cities, such as New York's City Volunteer Corps and Boston's City Year (Goldsmith, 1993).

The communal work being done by NYSC cadets in remote villages in the post-traumatized Nigeria; or the various psycho-social projects executed by teams of volunteers in earthquake-stricken areas such as Kobe, Japan; Armenia; and Turkey; as well as the numerous volunteer activities initiated following the southeast Asia tsunami of 2004, are all examples of youth volunteers enhancing social capital and community resilience following a major disaster. Among the major international aid bodies with which young volunteers work are the UNICEF, Medecins Sans Frontieres, Catholic Relief Service, the Red Cross and the Red Crescent.

In many countries, where ethnic or religious minorities are problematic, the volunteer youth organizations, comprised of mixed youth from all demographic categories, become a most effective melting-pot mechanism to minimize civil tension and promote common identity (Eberly and Sherraden, 1990). Such is the case, for example, with the Canadian Katimavik organization (where youth of French and English background serve together in different provinces), or Nigeria's NYSC (where students from different and sometimes rival tribes serve together). Only recently in Israel young Jews and Arabs in mixed volunteer groups have started to serve together with the aim of easing political and religious tension within the society. This will be further elaborated in the following sections.

But how does social capital become a strengthening force for community reconstruction?

There is a huge body of literature [see for example: Putnam, 1993(a); 1993(b); Coleman, 1990], covering many field research and systematic observations, that provides a good answer to this question. It is clearly evident that these civic engagements and social connections called social capital produce better schools, faster economic development, lower crime rates and more effective government services. Furthermore, social capital was found to be associated with people's health and with the welfare of children (Putnam, 2000). In short, all these findings show that life is easier in a community blessed with a substantial stock of social capital; its members share higher mutual trust and collaboration and exhibit higher levels of well-being.

Citizenship Behavior. Although not as operationally defined as 'social capital', Citizenship behavior is marked, first of all, by one's active participation in public affairs within one's community (Walzer, 1980). This modern notion of the citizenship concept is, indeed, a diversion from the more traditional notion of *republican citizenship*, embedded in the classical republics of Greece and Rome, emphasizing loyalty toward the homeland and the predominance of civic duties as its main principles. In contrast, the *liberal tradition* of Citizenship, originating in the philosophy of Locke and Jefferson, focuses more on the freedoms and rights of the citizen, and emphasizes civic involvement and responsibilities more than it does civic duties and obligations.

Stemming from this perspective, citizenship behavior means, first of all, "being familiar with the basic tenets of [one's] state and respecting them, especially those tenets concerning the effective working of a democracy: the separation of powers, the supremacy of the law, the democratic procedure for electing a government and for legislating, and for reviewing government activities" (Hareven, 1996).

Another expression of a liberal version of Citizenship Behavior is civic responsibility and civic initiative. These initiatives can take place in many fields, such as politics, economic enterprise, environmental protection, civil rights, education and culture. Finally, a higher level of citizenship behavior may involve caring for other citizens' misery and attending to others' needs. An apparent reflection of such expressions or implications is the growing expansion of non-governmental organizations (NGOs) in many democratic countries. The proliferation of such NGOs, and of citizenship involvement in general, transmit a clear message that "in a civil society not everything depends on government, but citizens can assume a great deal of initiative for change, independently of government, or in cooperation with it." (Hareven, 1996) (note 2)

And this is exactly the raison d'etre of most NYS programs: the notion that as a young citizen, and just before one is going to devote several years of one's life to one's own development – whether through higher education, job training or other self-interest initiatives, it will be the right "citizenship behavior" to devote a year or two of one's time and energy to the society, in the form of volunteering for NYS. And while the society undoubtedly gains, the benefits for the youth are also apparent.

Citizenship behavior, thus, results both in a stronger and more effective community, as well as in individuals who feel a sense of empowerment and self-efficacy.

Service-Learning. "Civil society will not survive without a new generation of engaged citizens. Bringing up youth with more entertainment or possessions has produced neither gratitude nor enlightenment. Regulating and controlling has led to rebellion and destructive acts. Dead-end jobs paying little and teaching less are not the answer ... [only] the wisdom of combining service and schooling ... provides a better path". (Kielsmeier, 1998; p.28). These were the fervent words of James C. Kielsmeier, one of the world's leaders of service-learning. Service-learning, as described in detail in Chapter 5, is a form of experiential education that combines structured opportunities for learning academic skills, reflection on the normative dimensions of civic life, and experiential activity that addresses community needs or assists individuals, families, and communities in need. (Hunter, 2000)

As noted before, service-learning programs are widespread today at all levels of educational institutions, from kindergartens to universities.(note 5). Typically, students at all levels rank these programs as one of the most significant parts of their overall education (Gray et. al., 1999). Furthermore, participating in service-learning programs results in students changing their perceptions of democratic governance and the practice of politics, in their willingness to and actual joining in voluntary activities, and in enhancing their sense of competence and commitment. For illustration, here is one example:

> Thammasat University in Thailand instituted the Graduate Volunteer Diploma Program in 1969. Its aim is to help cadets "see their service in the larger context of social justice and social policy rather than simple charity." Following four months of classroom study related to sociology and rural development, cadets serve for seven months in rural areas on projects related to such topics as nutrition and soil improvement. The service period includes five days to get together with fellow cadets to reflect on the service experiences, and after service cadets submit a mini-thesis integrating their classroom studies with the learning gained from their field experiences. In 2002, the Thai government was devising a plan to use the GVDP as the basis for engaging some 70,000 university graduates to serve as development volunteers. (Rattanamuk, 2003)

To summarize, then, we are facing an impressive phenomenon, where the expanding implementation of service-learning programs in various educational institutions throughout the world has transformed thousands of students from passive members to active participants, from help-seekers to help-providers, and from victims to leaders (Eberly & Kielsmeier, 1991).

An Israeli Example

Israel *is a* state under the pressure of continuous wars and struggles. While the repeated wars are between Israel and its Arab neighbors, the struggles within are mostly related to Israel's diverse population and minorities. Twenty percent of the populations of the Jewish state of Israel are Arabs (both Muslims and Christians). Although citizens, these Israeli Arabs are not allowed to serve in the Israeli conscription-based military (Gal & Sherraden, 1990), nor do they enjoy full-equal rights. This abnormal situation has generated repeated tensions throughout the years.

Only since the mid-1990s, a major effort has been launched to include Arab youth (age 18-22) in existing frameworks of voluntary youth service (Gal, 1999). Still in small numbers, most of these Arab volunteers (predominantly women) serve within their communities, among their own people. A small number, however, have preferred to serve in mixed teams together with Jewish women. Researchers at Carmel Institute were prompt to interview these young volunteers, as it was the first year (2000-2001) of such experimentation (note 6). All the volunteers who served together attested to the change in their attitudes and stereotypes towards the "others," and the impact that serving together had on viewing their colleagues (of the other ethnic group) as individuals, first.

> As one Arab girl who, after initial apprehensiveness of serving in a Jewish school and being the only Arab, summarized: "Everyone is equal, and we must move on with life, move past the political situation and continue with our lives".
> Several Arab girls reported that serving together "turns your head upside down", that it helps very much to changes stigmas and stereotypes. One Jewish girl said about her close Arab friend serving with her: "before anything, she is an individual." (RG)

Arab girls who reported on successful integration into the Jewish setting (school, kindergarten), expressed a sense of connection to the State and a sense of the importance of their contributions, as well as a feeling of being accepted by the greater society and positive feelings about their contributions to it.

> The Arab volunteers speak about their desire to feel as part of the country, an attachment to the country, that they gained through their service. As one girl explained: "The actual 'doing' of the national service gave me a certain connection to the country, a connection which is no longer expressed in words only." (RG)

One should keep in mind that these testimonies were made only six months after some terrible clashes occurred between police forces and Arab citizens, in the northern region ('Galil') of Israel. Thirteen Israeli-Arabs were killed in these riots, many were wounded and almost all were traumatized. Yet, mixed community service prevailed, and hopefully will further expand, to create a civil bridgehead towards communal recovery and co-existence.

Conclusion

Regional tensions, civil wars, and ethnic conflict – as well as natural disasters (such as earthquakes and floods) – are usually handled by military forces or political interventions, on the one hand, or by professional health-care givers, on the other. It is suggested that another resource, that of NYS, be brought to bear in these situations and that all of those involved in rescue, relief and rehabilitation act in a way that utilizes the concepts of social capital, service-learning, and citizenship behavior. These resources, in turn, can be expected to develop and empower local forces (e.g. lay leaders, social networks, and support-groups) in the crisis-aftermath phase, and thus become a crucial leverage for community reconstruction.

*   *   *   *   *

Though the strength of the entire chain is usually determined by the strength of its weakest link, when it comes to recovering communities the reverse is true, no less: The strength and well-being of each and every member of the community may be determined by the health and wealth of the encompassing community. The still-developing concepts of social capital, citizenship behavior, and service-learning can contribute to the post-stress recovery of communities and of nations.

Notes

(1) Special thanks to Simon Caplan and Nancy Shtreichman, members of the Carmel Institute staff, for their significant help.

(2) This involvement was generously initiated by the United Kingdom Jewish Aid and International Development (UK-JAID). See : "Helping the Helpers - The Record of UKJAID's Humanitarian Initiative in the former Yugoslavia 1992-1997." UKJAID, London (undated).

(3) James Coleman deserves primary credit for developing the "social capital" theoretical framework See: Coleman 1988; 1990. Apparently, the first scholar to use the term "social capital" in its current sense was Jane Jacobs, in *The Death and Life of Great American Cities* (New York: Random House, (1961). 138.

(4) This feeling of safety for little children was true in Jerusalem even during the turbulent days of another *Intifada* (civil uprising) in the summer of 2001. Apparently, social-capital assets are not that easily erased by political turbulence.

(5) Just as an illustration, the number of school students, in the U.S.A., engaged in service-learning in the year 1999 was 23.5 million. The growth in this number between 1984 and 1997 was 3663 percent.

(6) Special thanks and appreciation go to Nancy Shtreichman, who conducted these interviews.

CHAPTER 10

PRACTICAL MEASURES TO ADVANCE NATIONAL YOUTH SERVICE

During the second half of the 20th Century, many countries moved from conscription to a volunteer military, and many of those which retained conscription made provision for conscientious objection and alternative civilian service (ACS). Also, a number of countries introduced NYS programs unrelated to military service. As countries discover the value of NYS through their experiences with ACS or with other service programs, they may wish to institute NYS as a major public policy. What measures can they take to ensure that NYS has both positive and substantial impact on society and on the lives of young people?

Such countries will have to go beyond NYS programs like the Volunteer Years in Germany and AmeriCorps in the United States. Although they are well-designed, well-run, make significant service impacts, assist the personal growth and maturity of cadets, and have the incentive of educational benefits attached to the service, their participation rates are small. AmeriCorps attracts about one percent of the youth cohort in the USA and the Volunteer Years in Germany two percent of the female youth cohort. Those figures pale in comparison to the 20 percent of young German men in Zivildienst and the nearly 100 percent of university graduates in Nigeria's NYSC.

What is needed is the acceptance of NYS as a responsibility of citizenship. We think that Lincoln Myers, former Minister of National Service and the Environment in Trinidad & Tobago, hit the nail on the head when he said in reference to NYS that if democracy is to endure, "a balance must be struck between individual liberty and social responsibility, self-reliance and cooperation, private interest and public duty. It is this balance which provides the essential meaning of citizenship and nation-building." (Myers, 1991)

In many countries, particularly those in Europe and Latin America, the operative word is solidarity. According to Maria Nieves Tapia, Director of the Latin American Center for Service-Learning in Argentina, "'Solidaridad' means helping others in an organized and effective way, means working together for the common cause, means standing as a group or as a Nation to defend your rights, to face natural disasters or economic crisis, and to do it hand in hand. It is a word strongly related to the concept of 'fraternity ('hermandad': brotherhood/sisterhood, meaning you recognize humankind as a family, and you act in consequence.)" (Tapia, 2002) As such solidarity would seem to be virtually identical to the English word "Citizenship" which "has meant, since the time of the Greeks and the Romans, people acting together to achieve a reasonably important common purpose." (Crick, 2002)

As members of the public and politicians perceive that NYS cadets are advancing societies through the work they do and the experiences they have and the learnings they acquire, they will embrace NYS as they have embraced policies such as universal education and universal health care. When that happens, NYS will be seen as a responsibility of citizenship or an expression of solidarity. The challenge now is to develop strategies that will enable NYS to demonstrate its potential in a variety of settings.

It is worth noting that the NYS participation rate of a youth cohort will probably never exceed 75 percent. A number of people of NYS age will be in the military, the police force, the prisons; some will be unable to serve because of severe mental or physical disability; others will refuse to serve for religious or philosophical reasons. Once cadets comprise about one-quarter of the youth cohort, NYS will be well-enough known to public and politicians for them to make sound decisions about its further development. Several strategies that are realistic and can move a country from a small

NYS to one that reaches the one-quarter stage are suggested below.

Declare war on behalf of a great cause. There is a lesson to be learned from the military service experience. During the 20th Century, young men in the millions volunteered with great enthusiasm to join the military campaigns of Great Britain, Germany, Russia, China, Japan, the United States and many other countries. Already in the 21st Century, we have seen warlike passions aroused in young people in Israel and Palestine, in Iraq and the United States, in India and Pakistan.

Can such passions be harnessed for constructive service? Fidel Castro declared war on illiteracy in Cuba in 1961 and mobilized thousands of young people to teach others to read and write. In less than one year, they reduced the illiteracy rate from 27 percent to five percent. Later in the decade, one million or more young Americans actively protested against the war in Vietnam, leading directly to America's withdrawal from that conflict. Youth is a time of idealism, and if young people believe a cause to be just, they will appear in large numbers to pursue it.

In addition to literacy, great goals could include immunization campaigns; good quality day care for all preschool age children; a new kind of nursing home where old people could spend their remaining days in the company of young people; and large-scale environmental campaigns that will yield clean air, lakes and rivers.

Conduct joint basic training courses for NYS and the military. One way to introduce some young people to NYS would be to apply the military model. Old army camps could be used for groups of a few hundred young people to have medical checkups, physical training, lessons in personal hygiene, map reading and the like. The courses would be several months in duration and include elements found in military training such as drills, long route marches, mess duty, classes in hygiene and first aid. The program would include exposure to NYS by engaging in a few short-term service activities such as environmental cleanups of parks and beaches, escorting inner-city kids to a soccer game, and visiting NYS projects.

While weapons would be banned from these courses, participants would be exposed to military life by visiting a military camp. They would also be informed of opportunities for both military and civilian service and instructed on the conditions of service. They would have Internet access to enable them to search for openings that might interest them and be able to sign up for entry to NYS or the military at the completion of training. They could then select a service assignment for which they qualify or, if there is neither desire nor obligation for further service, they could choose to go back home.

In addition to encouraging enlistment in civilian or military service, these joint training camps would help overcome the problem found in countries with a volunteer military. As volunteer military forces enlist relatively small fractions of the youth population who serve for long periods of time, there is potential danger of a professional military establishment getting out of touch with the civilian sector of society.

Cooperate with the military on humanitarian missions. The distinction between military and civilian service need not be as great as the media often suggest, as in the labeling of hawks and doves in relation to a war, or in the seeming dichotomy of conscientious objectors and soldiers. For example, the majority of the young men classified in America as conscientious objectors during World War II served as noncombatants with the armed forces, and many served on the front lines as medics and cooks.

An Emergency Relief Corps would offer a good opportunity for such cooperation. Cadets working in NYS conservation programs could be given specialized training in rescue and relief and be available on short notice to respond to natural disasters. The Air Force could supply the necessary transport for rapid response.

Peacekeeping missions around the world could employ a mix of NYS and military personnel (see Chapter 9), with the armed soldiers providing protection and the NYS cadets doing civilian work. The variety of activities is illustrated in this account of an interview with Corporal Paul Robertson of New Zealand, just returned from a six-month tour of duty with the United Nations peacekeeping force in East Timor in 2001: "Locals love the military presence because it is a big deterrent. It provides them with the opportunity to get on with their lives and rebuild what they have lost.... it can be the little things that make a difference such as when [his] company adopted one of the local schools, built a new playground, tidied it up and donated stationery." (Robertson, 2001)

Extend secondary school to age 18 and convert the senior year into the NYS Year. This way, it would be somewhat attached to the existing institution of education and would help to insure that service-learning is well-integrated into the NYS experience. A year of service is a good length for NYS. Eighteen is a good time for volunteering, as persons of that age are ready and often eager to leave home and attain a measure of independence, to explore, to have an adventure, and do something meaningful. The experience will help cadets make up their minds about a career and further education or training. And they will gain the respect of the older generation for becoming productive members of society.

A variation on this approach would be to incorporate a year of NYS into tertiary education programs. If the work done by cadets is well integrated with the students' studies, it would add no more than two or three months to the length of the course.

Allocate one percent of the national budget to NYS. 20th Century experience with NYS suggests that inadequate funding may be the biggest issue with NYS programs. Central government funding for Indonesia's Kuliah Kerja Nyata (KKN) was severely curtailed in the mid-1980s with the collapse in the price of oil, which at the time accounted for 90 percent of Indonesia's export earnings. Although KKN remained in the government's Five Year Plan, government funding was eliminated and universities were asked to bear the cost of KKN. The consequence was that some universities dropped KKN while others reduced the period of service and made other cutbacks.

We recommend that NYS be allocated one percent of the national budget. That seems to be a small figure but consider what that amount would mean to the size of NYS in the United States. America spent four percent of its budget on the Civilian Conservation Corps in the 1930s, an amount which enabled 30 percent of the young male population to enroll in the CCC. An allocation of only one percent of the budget in 2000 would have permitted one million young people to serve in AmeriCorps every year, or 25 percent of the youthful population

Currently, one of the highest rates of expenditure for NYS is found in Germany, where Zivildienst accounted for 0.45 percent of the federal budget in 2000. That amount supported some 120,000 cadets in Zivildienst, or about 20 percent of a single year male cohort.

Attach NYS to existing institutions. Attaching NYS to existing public entities at the national, provincial, and local levels would give it a ready-made framework within which to operate and would facilitate its acceptance by the public. Zivildienst operates on a large scale in Germany as it is attached to the accepted institution of military service. The CCC in America was attached to the government ministries responsible for conservation and forestry, with logistical help from the army. Approval by the United States Appeal Court of community service as a requirement for high school graduation probably would not have happened had it not been linked to education and described as being analogous to other curricular requirements.

Just about every public agency as well as NGOs in areas such as health, conservation, and education could extend their outreach and improve their services with a reliable cadre of NYS cadets.

Those in the fire service could instruct school children in fire safety measures and visit residences to install smoke detectors and advise residents on hazardous conditions. Those in the education service could serve as tutors and teacher aides and literacy instructors. Those in the housing service could assist old folks with simple home maintenance which the old folks are no longer able to do and which enable them to continue living at home.

A stand-alone NYS is not attached to anything. It must struggle for identity, acceptance, and most of all, a budget. Thus, it makes sense to link NYS to existing institutions.

Work with a Global or Regional Youth Service. The First World War led directly to the creation of international service programs that have endured through the years. Both Service Civile Internationale and the International Student Service (now World University Service) began in the 1920s by arranging for university students and others from several countries to help with the reconstruction of war-torn countries. Their premise is that all peoples are entitled to the knowledge and skills necessary to contribute to a more equitable world, and their mission is to foster human development and global understanding through education and training. At first, students served for brief periods during the summer vacation, but in later years these programs have facilitated longer-term placements as well.

The United Nations Volunteers (UNV) is a global service program but since its founding in 1971 most of its participants have been mid-level career people aged 30 to 50. UNV did make an opening to younger participants in 2000 with the decision to accept an Italian offer to place recent university graduates as UNV interns for one year of service outside of Italy.

These international programs, as well as the regional European Voluntary Service, have good reputations but each is quite small. If they were linked with sizable NYS programs like those in China, Nigeria, and Germany, and given appropriate support, there would be opportunities to more fully realize their mission of increased international cooperation and understanding.

Another approach is to use existing NYS programs as the bases of global and regional programs. Conservation is an appropriate area as limited language ability is needed. Cadets from existing conservation corps could be joined in multinational teams and serve together in places where resources are small and the need is large. Where people from several countries speak the same language, such as Spanish or English, multi-national teams could easily engage in a wider array of service activities.

A Middle East Regional Youth Service might resemble that proposed in 1995 by Reuven Gal. Young people from Egypt, Israel, Palestine, Jordan, Lebanon and Syria would serve together in teams working on projects involving water supplies, public health measures, and environmental protection. Gal's most ambitious vision is the creation of a Middle East version of the Appalachian Trail in the United States. The cross-regional trail would start in Egypt, at the Nile Delta, cross the Sinai Peninsula and the Palestinian Gaza Strip into the southern Israeli Negev desert and over the Jordanian hills, and continue all the way to the Iraqi border. The mixed teams working along this trail would not only experience a road without borders, but also a collective accomplishment without rivalry.

Conduct occasional highly visible projects, bringing NYS to the eyes of the public. NYS programs often attract little public notice because cadets serve in a variety of activities. Since its beginning in the mid-1980s, the New York City Volunteer Corps has assembled all its 400 or so cadets together for a day or two each year to focus on one task, such as cleaning a beach or rebuilding a vandalized playground in a ghetto area. It accomplishes an important task, attracts the television cameras and newspaper photographers, reminds the public of the work of NYS, and gives the cadets a sense of solidarity with one another.

Get financial support for NYS from business and commercial firms. Community Service Volunteers in Great Britain and City Year in the United States have been successful in convincing businesses that support for NYS is a good investment. Businesses have found that such contributions appear to put them on a high moral plane by claiming "corporate social responsibility." One often sees advertisements on television and in publications whose time or space is devoted almost entirely to their support of some NYS activity, with only a brief mention of the company's name and product.

Bringing the profit-making sector into the NYS effort further broadens the base of NYS and facilitates the subsequent employment of NYS cadets by those firms that support NYS projects.

Convince a major public figure to promote NYS. While the advocacy of NYS by visionaries like Mahatma Gandhi and William James has influenced the development of NYS, its support by major public figures is often decisive in its implementation. This was the case with the three major NYS programs in the United States in the 20th Century. The Civilian Conservation Corps was rushed through Congress by President Roosevelt shortly after he took office in 1933. The Peace Corps was created by an Executive Order of President Kennedy one month after he took office in 1961, and AmeriCorps and its parent body, the Corporation for National Service, were priority items for President Clinton and they were established in 1993, the same year he became President. Canada's Katimavik came into being in 1977 because of Prime Minister Pierre Trudeau's strong backing.

Give recognition and rewards to those who serve in NYS. Their most fitting reward is entitlement to a period of further education and training. Cadets come out of their experience with clearer ideas about career paths than when they entered NYS. They are eager to pursue them and many recognize a need for further education.

A Certificate of National Youth Service given to departing cadets is a good idea. It could include information such as dates served, the organization where service was given, the cadet's responsibilities, the skills acquired, and perhaps a statement by the cadet on his service experience.

Both public and private sector employers should be encouraged to recognize the value of the service experience when considering the employment of former cadets and when setting their salaries.

Maintain a complete record of the benefits of NYS. The public and the politicians deserve to know how their tax dollars are spent, and NYS cadets deserve to know the total impact of their common endeavors. First and foremost, it is the persons served. They are primarily the sick, the frail, the illiterate, the poor, the very young or very old, the mentally or physically disabled. The benefits of conservation work spread throughout society.

Private and public sector employers benefit from the good work habits and skills acquired by those in NYS who later go to work for them. Such employers can reduce their expenditures for staff training and their losses from staff turn-over.

The community benefits both from the services of NYS and by having young people occupied and less likely to get into trouble that would create additional costs for the police and fire departments.

Tertiary educational institutions benefit from getting students with clear ideas about their choice of courses to study and strong motivations to apply themselves to their educational pursuits.

The nation benefits from having given young people an investment in their country. Just as people are loyal to their families for having raised them and to their schools and universities for having educated them, NYS veterans would join with military veterans in having an enhanced sense of patriotism.

Monitoring and recording all the above-mentioned potential benefits will provide the necessary evaluation-- both summative and transformative -- about NYS effectiveness.

Analyze the impact of NYS on statistics for crime, illiteracy, poverty, and unemployment. The most thorough evaluations of NYS have been done in America, but as yet there has been no direct evidence that the work of NYS has reduced crime, illiteracy, poverty, or unemployment to a significant degree. It is only when NYS begins to impact on these statistics that it will be taken seriously and perceived to be an integral part of public policy, rather than a nice thing to do, or something that is being done because of draft inequities or high youth unemployment. We think that NYS will begin to have a measurable impact on these statistics when about 15 percent of the youth population participates in NYS.

Recognize assorted youth service programs as part of an integrated NYS. Many countries have multiple youth service programs that operate in isolation form one another and are not seen conceptually as NYS. Brazil's Programa Universidade Solidaria for university students, its Servicio Civil Volontario for unemployed young people, and its civilian programs of the military are in this category. If Brazil's soldiers and university students and unemployed young people were to perceive their service activities as manifestations of NYS, we would hypothesize that it would promote a sense of solidarity among those in service and would stimulate the creation of additional service activities that would fall within the framework of NYS.

Develop NYS as a profession and as an academic discipline. As has happened with both environmental and women's studies in recent decades, so can NYS become an independent academic discipline, recognized as such in colleges and universities around the world. NYS can also be studied in the context of several related areas, such as psychology, sociology, education, gerontology, and international relations. The creation of NYS study programs would enrich our understanding of the NYS phenomenon – its motivations, effectiveness, long-term impact etc. -- and would also help to produce persons well-qualified to run NYS at all levels. Also, there are numerous lines of research that should be pursued. As examples, economists could examine the average value of the benefits for those who serve in NYS, psychologists could examine the effects of having NYS teams comprised of cadets from very different backgrounds, and sociologists could examine the relative merits of cadets serving in their home towns versus serving far away from them.

Keep NYS up-to-date. Like nearly everything else, NYS must change with the times and there are various techniques for doing that. Since its inception in 1961 the American Peace Corps has had a five-year rule which limits the employment of senior and middle management staff to no more than five years. The rationale behind this rule was to keep the Peace Corps from becoming too set in its ways and resistant to change.

Nigeria conducted a major review of its National Youth Service Corps in 2002. The program had grown to over 100,000 from 2,363 at its founding in 1973. Also, there had been a recent shift from a military government to an elected government and with it, the transfer of responsibility from the Army to the Federal Ministry of Women Affairs and Youth

Development. (Federal Ministry, 2002) The government sub-sequently adopted many of the recommendations.

*   *   *   *   *

Given the promise of National Youth Service, it is clear to us that the idea will be with us for many generations to come. The question is the extent to which the NYS idea will find expression as a common experience of young people around the world. The decision will be made by today's young people and those who follow them. If young people in the 21st Century have as much experience with NYS as their forebears had with military service in the 20th Century, we are confident they will make the right decisions.

CHAPTER 11

CONCLUSION

To a large extent in recent centuries, employment has replaced serfdom and slavery, education of the masses has replaced boarding schools for the few, and democracy has replaced dictatorships and colonial domination. It now appears that military service is being replaced to some degree by various forms of civic service. Given the constructive impacts of NYS on those who are served, on the cadets who serve, and on communities and nations, that is a trend that should be continued within the boundaries of quality control.

The provision of services to persons in need and to the environment has not kept pace with the rapid changes in technology, in society, and in governments. By the turn of the century, NYS programs in various parts of the world had progressed sufficiently to convince us that NYS has the potential to fill a substantial part of the gap in the provision of services to needy persons and to the environment.

As has been demonstrated time and again, NYS cadets can teach people to read and write; provide safe drinking water, improve the environment; advise adolescents on good health practices; and can nurture children in day care, old folks living alone and in nursing homes, and persons who are mentally retarded or mentally ill. Based on what the two of us have studied and experienced over nearly 100 years of combined interest in NYS, we are confident that NYS programs, when properly designed and properly administered, can be expected to yield the following set of outcomes.

NYS is good value for money. Simply in terms of services rendered by cadets to persons in need and to the environment, we can expect the value of those services to exceed the cost of the program. From the Poverty Alleviation Relay Project in China, to the National Service Scheme in India, to the Pakistan National Youth Service, to Sherut Leumi in Israel, to the National Civil Service of Italy, to Zivildienst in Germany, to Community Service Volunteers in the UK, to the National Youth Service Corps of Nigeria, to the National Service Scheme in Ghana, to Servicio Pais in Chile, to AmeriCorps in the USA and Katimavik in Canada, NYS cadets are making cost-effective contributions to their countries and to humankind.

NYS provides substantial benefits to the cadets who serve. They include work experience, career exploration, skills acquired, increased social maturity and self-esteem, increased awareness of the needs of others, and new understanding between ages, races, ethnic, and linguistic groups. For many cadets the service experience is a rite of passage from adolescence to adulthood. The profile of benefits is different for each cadet, but if we could quantify them and add them up, we are fairly confident that the total value would be greater than program costs and – over a cadet's lifetime -- greater that the value of services rendered. It is this accumulation of benefits to the cadets that prevents national service from becoming an exploitative program. While cadets' dollar incomes are below market wages, the sum of their psychic income and the value of their long-term benefits more than make up the difference.

NYS operates successfully on a large scale. There are any number of small youth programs that have been successful, perhaps because of a particularly-talented leader or an unique local situation, but that is not sufficient proof that they can function well on a large scale. With NYS, we have seen successful large-scale operation with programs such as the

Civilian Conservation Corps in the USA, Zivildienst in Germany, Sherut Leumi in Israel, the National Youth Service Corps in Nigeria, and the National Service Scheme in Ghana.

NYS contributes to nation-building. By giving a year or two of service cadets feel they have made an investment in their country. That encourages them to develop strong national loyalties and a deep sense of citizenship, as has been true with military veterans over the years. A service period also gives cadets a better understanding of communal needs and national issues, and that understanding can be expected to influence cadets as they choose careers and engage in civic pursuits.

It is likely that both communities and nations benefit from an increase in social capital and a reduction in crime, savings on welfare, unemployment payouts, and training courses. As yet, we do not have adequate research on these factors. Thus, experiences with NYS in the 20th Century suggest that, in terms of the needs of individual countries, of society-at-large, and of young people the world over, NYS can successfully replace military service to a substantial extent. It could become in the 21st Century as much an institution of society as military service was in the 20th Century.

* * * * *

Now, how do we get from where we were at the turn of the Century to this rather utopian world where military service is on the decline while NYS is on the rise, where most young people are happily and constructively engaged in serving others and the environment? Chapter 10 describes a number of practical measures that countries can take to advance NYS, but we believe that NYS is better viewed in the long run as deriving from a larger ethos.

Perhaps NYS will be viewed as a manifestation of a service contract between a state and its young people. If NYS is to operate on a large scale throughout the world, there will have to be forms of the service contract which build NYS into the life of a country and of young people as integrally as the study of anatomy is woven into medical education. Just as the medical profession and aspiring doctors recognize the importance of knowledge of anatomy to becoming a doctor, both society-at-large and young people would recognize the importance of a period of service to becoming a good citizen. That social contract will vary among countries, as there are different norms on matters such as individual choice, collective responsibility, remuneration, and acceptable kinds of service.

Perhaps history will see NYS as a manifestation of citizenship along the lines suggested by Pierluigi Consorti as he traces the evolution of National Civil Service (NCS) in Italy. Beginning with required military service and moving in stages through a rather punitive alternative civilian service (ACS), to an ACS on a level with military service, and then to the end of military conscription and introduction of NCS, Consorti describes the evolution as a part of the shift in the perception of citizenship. From the old idea of a people being subject to a State, nowadays, he says, citizenship concerns the forms of mutual relationships between single persons and the community that represents them.

Perhaps NYS will be seen in most countries as an expression of solidarity, in which young people join together in common cause to serve the environment and persons in need.

Call it a social contract. Call it citizenship. Call it solidarity. We believe that the promise and potential of NYS will be realized when states recognize their responsibility to encourage young people to serve and to support them in their service, when parents and communities and educational institutions and businesses and religious bodies recognize their responsibility to foster service by young people, and when young people themselves recognize their responsibility as members of a civil society to contribute a period of service. Above all, we believe that the 21st Century can be the beginning of an era when wars and military service may be replaced to a significant degree with National Youth Service. That is why we have called this book *Service Without Guns*.

REFERENCES

Part I: Inter-relationship of Military Service and Civic Service

1 Military Service at the Beginning of the 21st Century

Citizen's army to flex babu muscle. *Asia-Africa Intelligence Wire (AAIW)*, Aug. 26, 2002.

Haltiner, W. Karl (1998), The Definite End of the Mass Army in Western Europe, *Armed Forces and Society*, Vol. 25, No. 1, Fall 1998, pp. 7-36.

Haltiner, W. Karl (2001), *Mass Army Survey 1970-2000*. (Updated 2001 by Dr. S Haumssler).

Haltiner, Karl W. & Szvircsev Tresch, Tibor (2005). *The Decline of Conscription in Europe*. In: Bebler, Anton (ur.) (2005). Sodobno Vojaštvo in Družba. Fakulteta za družbene vede (Knjižna zbirka Varnostne študije), Ljublijana.

James, William The Moral Equivalent of War, in *Essays on Faith and Morals* (1910), New York: Longman, Greens, 1943, pp. 311-28.

The International Institute for Strategic Studies, *The Military Balance 2000-2001*, Oxford University Press, October 2000.

Military Draft: Volunteers filling the ranks. *Bangkok Post*, April 16, 2001. pp. 14-31.

Moskos Charles C. (2000): Toward a Postmodern Military: The United State as a Paradigm, in Moskos, Charles C., Segal, David R. Segal & John A. Williams (eds.), *The Post-Modern Military: Armed Forces after the Cold War*, NY: Oxford University Press, 2000, pp. 14-31.

Moskos, Charles C., David R. Segal & John A. Williams (2000): Armed Forces After the Cold War, in Moskos Charles C., Segal, David R. Segal & Williams John A. Williams (eds.), *The Post-Modern Military: Armed Forces after the Cold War*, NY: Oxford University Press, 2000

Von-Bredow, Wilfried (1999): "New Roles for Armed Forces and the Concept of Democratic Control, " Paper presented to the Biennial Conference of the Inter-University Seminar on Armed Forces and Society (IUS), Baltimore, MD (USA), October 22-24, 1999.

Weiss, Thomas G. & Kurt M. Campbell (1991): Military Humanitarianism, *Survival*, Vol. 33, No. 5, September/October 1991, pp. 451-465.

2 Linkages between Civic and Military Service in the 20th Century

Akpan, Edet A, Valedictory Address of Dec. 19, 1987, in *NYSC: Twenty Years of National Service*, ed. Gregory Enegwea and Gabriel Umoden (Lagos, Nigeria: Gabumo Publishing Company, Ltd., 1993) p.295.

Chambers, John Whiteclay, Conscientious Objectors and the American State from Colonial Times to the Present, in *The New Conscientious Objector*, op cit. p.27.

Eberly Donald J, ed., *National Youth Service: A Global Perspective* (Washington, DC, National Service Secretariat: 1992) p.38.

Gal, Reuven, *Community-Civic Service in Israel*, (Zikhron Ya'akov, Israel: Carmel Institute for Social Studies, 1995) p. 1.

Glick, Edward Bernard. *Peaceful Conflict: The Non-military Uses of the Military*. Harrisburg, PA: Stackpole Books, 1967, pp. 33-34.

James, William, The Moral Equivalent of War, *The Writings of William James*, John J. McDermott, Ed. (New York, The Modern Library: 1968) p. 669.

James, William, *op cit.*, p. 668-669.

Janowitz, Morris, American Democracy and Military Service. *TransAction*. No. 4, (March 1967): 59.

Johnson, Lyndon, *National Service Newsletter*. No. 3, October 1966, National Service Secretariat, Washington, DC, p. 1.

Kuhlmann Jurgen and Ekkehard Likkert, The Federal Republic of Germany: Conscientious Objection as Social Welfare, in *The New Conscientious Objection*, ed. Charles C. Moskos and John Whiteclay Chambers II (New York: Oxford University Press, 1993), 98.

Kuhlmann Jurgen, West Germany: The Right Not to Bear Arms, in *The Moral Equivalent of War: A Study of Non-Military Service in Nine Nations*. Eds. Donald Eberly and Michael Sherraden (Westport, CT: Greenwood Press, 1990), p. 146.

Kuhlmann Jurgen (citation), The Right Not to Bear Arms, in *The Moral Equivalent of War: A Study of Non-Military Service in Nine Nations*, op. cit., pp 147-148.

Michigan State News, Peace Corps – Wishful Thinking, Editorial of January 25, 1961, *A Profile of National Service*, Ed. Donald J. Eberly (New York: Overseas Educational Service: 1966) p. 51.

Ponomarenko, Tanya, of Sozidanie Foundation, Moscow, ACS in Russia, email message to Donald Eberly of March 2, 2001.

Rosenstock-Huessy, Eugen, *Planetary Service*, (Norwich, Vermont: Argo Books, 19780, p. 42.

Sani, Alhaji Garba Young People's Experiences and Views, *National Youth Service into the 21st Century, The Report of the 4th Global Conference on National Youth Service.* ed. Bridie Duffy (London: Community Service Volunteers, 1998) p. 44.

Sherraden, Michael W. and Donald J. Eberly, The Economic Value of Service Projects, *National Service: Social, Economic and Military Impacts*, Michael W. Sherraden and Donald J. Eberly eds., (New York, Pergamon Press: 1982) pp. 164-169.

Testing for the Draft, *The New York Times*, May 14, 1966, p.30.

Part II: What is National Youth Service all about?

3 Trends Toward National Youth Service

Chambers II, John Whiteclay, Conscientious Objectors and the American State from Colonial Times to the Present, in Charles C. Moskos and John Whiteclay Chambers II, *The New Conscientious Objection.* Oxford University Press, New York City: 1993, p. 33.

Chibber, M. L., *National Service for Defence, Development and National Integration of India.* Kartikeya Publications, Meerut, India, 1995.

Mweene, Joseph Miti, Zambia, *National Youth Service into the 21st Century: The Report of the 4th Global Conference on National Youth Service.* Ed. Bridie Duffy, (Community Service Volunteers, London: 1998) p. 25.

Palazzini, Licio, The National Service in Italy: History, Legislation and the Future, Paper presented at the Innovations in Civic Participation conference in Rome, March 16, 2002.

Wofford, Harris, Message to the Conference from Harris Wofford, CEO of the Corporation for National Service, USA, *National Youth Service into the 21st Century: The Report of the 4th Global Conference on National Youth Service.* Ed. Bridie Duffy (Community Service Volunteers, London: 1998) p. 12.

4 Best Practices of National Youth Service

Federal Ministry of Women Affairs and Youth Development, *Report of the Technical Committee on the Re-Organisation of the National Youth Service Corps (NYSC).* Federal Ministry of Women Affairs and Youth Development, Abuja, Nigeria, 2002.

Kappa Systems, Inc., *The Impact of Participation in the Program for Local Service.* (Kappa Systems, Inc., Arlington, Virginia: 1975.

Korten, David C. and Frances F. Korten, The Impact of a National Service Experience Upon Its Participants: Evidence from Ethiopia, *Comparative Review* 13, no.3 (October 1969): 312-324.

5 The Special Case of Service-Learning

Atlanta Service-Learning Conference, *Atlanta Service-Learning Conference Report*. Southern Regional Education Board, Atlanta: 1970, p.2.

Eberly, Donald, Only One Goal in It, *The Times Educational Supplement*. London: August 4, 1978.

Gal, Reuven, Editor, quoting Maria Nieves Tapia on National Youth Service in Argentina, *The Role of National Youth Service in Building Citizenship and Society*. (Jerusalem: 2000: Carmel Institute for Social Studies), p.41.

Havighurst, Robert J., Richard A. Graham, Donald Eberly, American Youth in the Mid-Seventies, *Bulletin of the National Association of Secondary School Principals*. Vol. 56, No. 367, November 1972.

Hardjasoemantri, Koesnadi, *Study-Service as a Subsystem in Indonesian Higher Education*. Jakarta, Indonesia: PN BALAI PUSTAKA, 1982.

Kielsmeier, James C., Peter Scales, Eugene C. Roehlkepartain and Marybeth Neal, Preliminary Findings Community Service and Service-Learning in Public Schools, *Growing to Greatness 2004*. (National Youth Leadership Council, St. Paul, Minnesota: 2004) 6-8.

Nyerere, Julius, Tanzania Ten Years after Independence, Cited in *Education with Production: The Journal of the Foundation for Education with Production*. Vol 9, No. 1, Nov. 1992, 50

Pinkau, Irene, *Service for Development*. Dayton, Ohio: Charles F. Kettering Foundation, 1978.

Tapia, Maria Nieves Service Learning in Latin America. *Aprender Sirve, Servir Ensena*. Latin American Center for Service-Learning, Buenos Aires: 2002, p. 8.

Part III: The Impact of National Youth Service

6 National Youth Service as a Psycho-Social Process

Arnett, J.J. (1998). Learning to stand alone: The contemporary American transition to adulthood in cultural and historical context. *Human Development*, 41. 295-315.

Arnett, J.J. (2000). Emerging Adulthood: A Theory of Development from the Late Teens through the Twenties. *American Psychologist*, 55(5), 469-480.

Bandura, A. (1977). Self-efficacy: Toward a unifying theory of behavioral change. *Psychological Review*, 84(2), 191-215

Bandura, A. (1982). Self-efficacy mechanism in human agency. *American Psychologist*, 37(2), 122-147.

Barnhill, L. R., & Longo, D. (1978). Fixation and regression in the family life cycle. *Family Process*, 17, 469-478.

Corporation for National Service. (1997). *Making a Difference: Impact of AmeriCorps State/National Direct on Members and Communities 1994-95 and 1995-96*. Aguirre International, San Mateo, CA.

Duval, E. M.(1985). *Family Development*. Philadelphia: J.B. Lippincott Co.

Endler, N. S. & Summerfeldt, L. J. (1995). Intelligence, Personality, Psychopathology, and Adjustment. In: Saklofske, D. H. and Zeidner, M. (Eds.) *International Handbook of Personality and Intelligence*. New York: Plemun Press.

Erikson, E. H. (1950). *Childhood and Society*. New York: Norton.

Erikson, E. H. (1968). *Identity: Youth and Crisis*. New York: Norton.

Ferreira, M. (2000). Voluntary Work as a Psycho-social Process. Paper prepared for the *5th Global Conference of IANYS*, Jerusalem, Israel.

Gardner, H. (1982). *Developmental Psychology* (2d ed.). Boston: Little, Brown.

Gardner, H. (1983). *Frames of mind: The theory of multiple intelligences*. New York: Basic Books.

Katimavik (no authors' name/s) (1999). *Evaluation Report*. Katimavik, Montreal, Canada.

Maslow, A. H. (1968). *Toward a Psychology of Being*. New York: Van Nostrand Reinhold.

Maslow, A. H. (1971). *The farther reaches of the human mind*. New York: Viking.

Rindfuss, R. R. (1991). The young adult years: Diversity, structural change, and fertility. Demography, 28, 493-512

Rotter, J. (1966). Generalized expectancies for internal versus external control of reinforcement. *Psychological Monographs*, 80, 1-28.

Rotter, J. (1975). Some problems and misconceptions related to the construct of internal versus external control of reinforcement. *Journal of Consulting and Clinical Psychology*, 43, 56-57.

Sternberg, R. J. (1990). *Metaphors of mind: Conceptions of the nature of intelligence*. New York: Cambridge University Press.

7 The Service Impact of National Youth Service

Aguirre International (1997). *Making a Difference: Impact of AmeriCorps State/National Direct on Members and Communities 1994-95 and 1995-96.* Corporation for National Service, Washington, DC p 142.

Elicegui, Pablo. *Argentina: Country Report to IANYS 7GC.* Ministry of Education, Science and Technology and Center for Service-Learning in Latin America. 2004.

Enegwea, Gregory and Gabriel Umoden. <u>*NYSC: Twenty Years of National Service.*</u> Lagos, Nigeria: National Youth Service Corps Directorate Headquarters 1993. Pp. 162-174.

Etude Economique Conseil. *Evaluation of the Economic and Social Impacts of the Katimavik Program* April 2002. Pp. 2-3.

Fleischer, Nicole. The Carmel Institute for Social Studies, Israel 2004. *National Youth Service in Israel: A Summary of Research.*

Huessy, Hans, quoted in Coalition for National Service, *National Service: an Action Agenda for the 1990s.* (National Service Secretariat, Washington, DC) 1988, p.3.

Kappa Systems, Inc., *The Impact of Participation in the Program for Local Service.* (Kappa Systems, Inc., Arlington, Virginia: 1975.

Kuhlmann, Jurgen, "The Right Not to Bear Arms," *The Moral Equivalent of War: A Study of Non-Military Service in Nine Nations.* Eds. Donald Eberly and Michael Sherraden (Westport, CT: Greenwood Press) pp. 147-148.

Nagar, Mahendra, "Youth for Nation Building," Report presented to the 7th Global Conference of IANYS, Accra, Ghana: 2004. pp. 2-5

Oki, Walter, "Country Update: The National Youth Service Corps – Nigeria," Report presented to the 7th Global Conference of IANYS, Accra, Ghana: 2004. p.6

Stringham, John. *International Voluntary Service in Europe – National and EU Policies.* Association of Voluntary Service Organisations, 2004.

Oki, Walter, "Country Update: The National Youth Service Corps – Nigeria," Report presented to the 7th Global Conference of IANYS, Accra, Ghana: 2004. p.6

Stringham, John. *International Voluntary Service in Europe – National and EU Policies.* Association of Voluntary Service Organisations, 2004.

8   National Youth Service as Strong Policy

Abt Associates (1996). *Impacts of Service: Final Report on the Evaluation of American Conservation and Youth Service Corps.* Cambridge, MA: Abt Associates.

Alexander, Jeffrey, ed., (1985). *Neofunctionalism*. Beverly Hills: Sage.
Allen, Joseph; Philliber, Susan; Herrling, Scott; & Kuperminc, Gabriel P. (1997). Article in *Child Development*.

Barber, Benjamin (1984). *Strong Democracy: Participatory Politics for a New Age*. Berkeley: University of California Press.

Beverly, Sondra, and Sherraden, Michael (1999). Institutional Determinants of Savings: Implications for Low-income Households, *Journal of Socio-Economics*.

Bollen, K.A. (1989). *Structural Equations with Latent Variables*. New York: Wiley.

Brent, Robert (1996). *Applied Cost-Benefit Analysis*. Cheltenham: Edward Elgar.

Cassel, John (1976). The Contribution of the Social Environment to Host Resistance, *American Journal of Epidemiology* 104, 107-123.

Coleman, James (1972). *Youth: Transition to Adulthood*, Report on Youth of the President's Science Advisory Committee. Chicago: University of Chicago Press.

Coleman, James (1976). The School to Work Transition, in U.S. Congressional Budget Office, *The Teenage Unemployment Problem: What Are the Options?* Washington: U.S. Government Printing Office, 35-40.

Coleman, James (1990). *Foundations of Social Theory*. Cambridge, MA: Harvard University Press.
Danzig, Richard, and Peter Szanton (1986). *National Service: What Would It Mean?* Lexington, MA: Lexington Books.

Dewey, John (1927). *The Public and Its Problems*. New York: Holt.

Durlauf, Steven N. (1999). The Case "Against" Social Capital, *Focus* 20(3), 1-5. Madison: University of Wisconsin, Institute for Research on Poverty.

Eberly, Donald (1970). *The Estimated Effect of a National Service Program on Public Service Manpower Needs, Youth Unemployment, College Attendance and Marriage Rates*. New York: Russell Sage Foundation, 1970.

Eberly, Donald (1986). National Youth Service in the 1990's, in Anthony Richards and Lidia Kemeny, eds., *Service Through Learning, Learning Through Service* No.1, Halifax, NS: Dalhousie University.

Eberly, Donald, and Sherraden, Michael, eds. (1990). *The Moral Equivalent of War? A Study of Non-Military Service in Nine Nations*. New York: Greenwood Press.

Enemuo, Francis (2000). Youth Mobilisation and Nation-Building: The Case of the National Youth Service Corps Scheme in Nigeria, paper prepared for the Worldwide Workshop on Youth Involvement as a Strategy for Social, Economic, and Democratic Development, sponsored by the Ford Foundation, San Jose, Costa Rica, January 4-7.

Erikson, Erik (1967). Memorandum for the Conference on the Draft, in Sol Tax, ed., *The Draft*, 280-283. Chicago: University of Chicago Press.

Espinoza, Vicente (2000). Youth Citizenship: Intellectual Foundation for a Youth Sector in Chile, paper prepared for the Worldwide Workshop on Youth Involvement as a Strategy for Social, Economic, and Democratic Development, sponsored by the Ford Foundation, San Jose, Costa Rica, January 4-7.

Etzioni, Amitai (1983). *An Immodest Agenda: Rebuilding America before the Twenty-First Century*. New York: McGraw-Hill.

Friedman, Milton (1979). Universal National Service, *Newsweek*, May 14, 101.

Gal, Reuven (2000). Israel's Multi-faceted National Youth Service: A Country Profile, paper prepared for the Worldwide Workshop on Youth Involvement as a Strategy for Social, Economic, and Democratic Development, sponsored by the Ford Foundation, San Jose, Costa Rica, January 4-7.

Glick, Edward (1967). *Peaceful Conflict: The Non-Military Use of the Military*. Harrisburg, PA: Stackpole Books.

Hage, Jerald (1972). *Techniques and Problems in Theory Construction in Sociology*. New York: John Wiley.

Hanning, Hugh (1967). *The Peaceful Uses of Military Forces*. New York: Praeger.

James, William (1910). The Moral Equivalent of War, *International Conciliation*, No. 27.

Jacoby, Barbara and Associates (1996). *Service Learning in Higher Education*. San Francisco: Jossey-Bass.

Janowitz, Morris (1975) Social Control and Macrosociology, *American Journal of Sociology* 81, 82-109.

Janowitz, Morris (1980). Observations on the Sociology of Citizenship, *Social Forces* 59(1), 1-24.

Janowitz, Morris (1983). *The Reconstruction of Patriotism: Education for Civic Consciousness*. Chicago: University of Chicago Press.

Joreskog, K., and Sorbom, D. (1993). *LISREL 8: Structural Equation Modelling with Simplis Command Language*. Chicago: Scientific Software International, Inc.

Krauskopf, Dina (2000). Youth Development, Participation, and Services, paper prepared for the Worldwide Workshop on Youth Involvement as a Strategy for Social, Economic, and Democratic Development, sponsored by the Ford Foundation, San Jose, Costa Rica, January 4-7.

Krugman, Paul (1995). *Development, Geography, and Economic Theory*. Cambridge, MA: MIT Press.

Latham, Earl (1958). *The Philosophy and Politics of Woodrow Wilson*. Chicago: University of Chicago Press.

Lieberson, Stanley (1985). *Making It Count: the Improvement of Social Research and Theory*. Berkeley: University of California Press.

Marshall, T.H. (1950). *Citizenship and Social Class*. Cambridge: Cambridge University Press.

Marshall, T.H. (1977). *Class, Citizenship, and Social Development*. Chicago: University of Chicago Press.

McLuhan, Marshall (1994). *Understanding Media: The Extension of Man*, reprint edition. Cambridge, MA: MIT Press.

Mead, Margaret (1967). A National Service System as a Solution to a Variety of National Problems, in Sol Tax, ed., *The Draft*, 99-109. Chicago: University of Chicago Press.

Midgley, James (1995). *Social Development*. Thousand Oaks, CA: Sage.

Morrow-Howell, Nancy; Hinterlong, James; and Sherraden, Michael, eds. (forthcoming). *Perspectives on Productive Aging*. Baltimore: Johns Hopkins University Press.

Moskos, Charles (1988). *A Call to Civic Service*. New York: Free Press, 1988.

Ninacs, William A., and Toye, Michael (2000). Canadian Youth Service Organizations, paper prepared for the Worldwide Workshop on Youth Involvement as a Strategy for Social, Economic, and Democratic Development, sponsored by the Ford Foundation, San Jose, Costa Rica, January 4-7.

Oliver, Melvin, and Shapiro, Thomas (1995). *Black Wealth/White Wealth*. New York: Routledge.

Page-Adams, Deborah, and Sherraden, Michael (1996). Asset Building as a Community Revitalization Strategy, *Social Work* 42(5): 423-434.

Park, Robert, and Burgess, Ernest (1921). *Introduction to the Science of Sociology*. Chicago: University of Chicago Press.

Parsons, Talcott (1951). *The Social System*. Glencoe, IL: Free Press.

Putnam, Robert (1993). *Making Democracy Work: Civic Traditions in Modern Italy*. Princeton, NJ: Princeton University Press.

Putnam, Robert (1995). Bowling Alone: The Strange Disappearance of Civic America, *Journal of Democracy* 6, 65-78.

Putnam, Robert (2000). Youth Service and Social Capital, opening plenary the Worldwide Workshop on Youth Involvement as a Strategy for Social, Economic, and Democratic Development, sponsored by the Ford Foundation, San Jose, Costa Rica, January 4-7.

Rosenstock-Huessy, Eugen (1978) [translated from the original 1965 German edition). *Planetary Service*. Norwich, VT: Argo.

Ruiz Duran, Clemente (2000). Reciprocity and Economics of Solidarity in the 21st Century: The Role of Youth, paper prepared for the Worldwide Workshop on Youth Involvement as a Strategy for Social,

Economic, and Democratic Development, sponsored by the Ford Foundation, San Jose, Costa Rica, January 4-7.

Schmitter, Philippe, and Lehmbruch, Gerhard eds. (1980). *Trends toward Corporatist Intermediation*. Beverly Hills: Sage.

Schreiner, Mark (1999). *A Cost-Effectiveness Analysis of the Grameen Bank of Bangladesh*, working paper 99-5. St. Louis: Center for Social Development, Washington University.

Saleeby, Dennis (1997). *The Strengths Perspective in Social Work Practice*, 2nd edition. New York: Longman.

Salmond, John A. (1967). *The Civilian Conservation Corps, 1933-1942: A New Deal Case Study*. Durham, NC: Duke University Press.

Sherraden, Margaret S., and Sherraden, Michael (1999). *Youth Service and Cross-Border Policy in North America*, presentation at "Advancing the North American Community: The Role of Community Service and Volunteering," sponsored by the North American Institute and the Ford Foundation, September 24-26.

Sherraden, Michael (1979). *The Civilian Conservation Corps: Effectiveness of the Camps*, doctoral dissertation. Ann Arbor: University of Michigan.

Sherraden, Michael (1980). Youth Employment and Education: Federal Programs from the New Deal through the 1970s, *Children and Youth Services Review* 2(1-2), 17-39.

Sherraden, Michael (1987). The Myth of the Youth Labor Shortage, *Social Policy* 17(3), 12-13.

Sherraden, Michael (1991a). Youth Participation in America: A Historical View of Changing Institutions, in Donald Eberly, ed., *National Youth Service: A Democratic Institution for the 21st Century*. Washington: National Service Secretariat.

Sherraden, Michael (1991b). *Assets and the Poor: A New American Welfare Policy*. Armonk, NY: M.E. Sharpe.

Sherraden, Michael (1998). *Community Development and Policy Innovation in a Time of Transition*, The John Roatch Global Lecture on Social Policy and Practice. Tempe, AZ: University of Arizona.

Sherraden, Michael (2000). *Asking Questions Well: The Role of Theory in Applied Social Research*, keynote address, Twelfth Annual Symposium on Doctoral Research in Social Work. Columbus: Ohio State University.

Sherraden, Michael (2001). Asset Building Policy and Programs for the Poor, in Thomas Shapiro and Edward N. Wolff, eds., *Benefits and Mechanisms for Spreading Asset Ownership in the United States*, 302-333. New York: Russell Sage Foundation.

Sherraden, Michael, and Adamek, Margaret (1984). Explosive Imagery and Misguided Policy, *Social Service Review*, 58(4), 539-555.

Sherraden, Michael, and Eberly, Donald (1984). Individual Rights and Social Responsibilities: Fundamental Issues in National Service, *Public Law Forum* 4(1), 241-257.

Sherraden, Michael; Sherraden, Margaret S.; & Eberly, Donald (1990). Comparing and Understanding Non-Military Service in Different Nations, in Eberly and Sherraden, eds., *The Moral Equivalent of War?*

Stepan, A. (1978). *The State and Society*. Princeton, NJ: Princeton University Press.

Tocqueville, Alexis de (1969) [originally published in 1835]. *Democracy in America*. Garden City, NY: Anchor Books.

Turner, Jonathan, and Maryanski, Alexandra (1988). Is `Neofunctionalism' Really Functional? *Sociological Theory* 6(1), 110-121.

Turner, Ralph (1967). *On Social Control and Collective Behavior*. Chicago: University of Chicago Press.

Ul Haq, Mahbub, and Streeten, Paul (1995). *Reflections on Human Development*. New York: Oxford University Press.

Weick, A.; Rapp, C.; Sullivan, W.P.; and Kisthardt, W. (1989). A Strengths Perspective for Social Work Practice, *Social Work* 34, 350-354.

White, Geoffrey (1978). *National Youth Service and Higher Education*. Boston: Sloan Commission on Government and Higher Education.

Wirtz, Willard, and the National Manpower Institute (1975). *The Boundless Resource: A Prospectus for an Education/Work Policy*. Washington: New Republic.

Woolcock, Michael (1998). Social Capital and Economic Development: Toward a Theoretical Synthesis and Policy Framework, *Theory and Society* 27, 151-208.

Yadama, Gautam, and Sherraden, Michael (1996). Effects of Assets on Attitudes and Behaviors: Advance Test of a Social Policy Proposal, *Social Work Research* 20(1), 3-11.

Yarmolinsky, Adam (1977). *National Service Program*, Final Report of the Senior Conference on National Compulsory Service. West Point, NY: U.S. Military Academy.

Part IV: Future of National Youth Service

9 Potential Role for National Youth Service in Community Reconstruction and International Understanding

Coleman, J.S. (1988). Social Capital in the Creation of Human Capital. *American Journal of Sociology* 94 (Supplement), S95-S120.

_____. (1990). *The Foundations of Social Theory*. Cambridge: Harvard University Press.

Eberly, D. and Sherraden, M. (1990). *The Moral Equivalent of War?* New York, Greenwood Press.

Eberly D. J. and Kielsmeier, J. C. (1991) National Youth Service: A Democratic Institution for the 21st Century, in Donald J. Eberly, (ed.) *National Youth Service: A Democratic Institution for the 21st Century.* Washington, DC: National Service Secretariat 31-46.

Gal, R. (1999). Israel's Multi-faceted National Youth Service : A Country Profile Paper . Paper presented at the Worldwide Workshop on Youth Service (Ford Foundation), Costa Rica.

Gal, R. and Sherraden, M. (1990). Israel: Non-Military Service Amidst Continuing Conflict, in D. Eberly and M. Sherraden (Eds.) *The Moral Equivalent of War ? A Study of Non-Military Service in Nine Nations.* Westport, CT: Greenwood Press.

Goldsmith, S. (1993) *A City Year.* The New Press, New York.

Gray et al. (1999) Combining Service and Learning in Higher Education. Evaluation of the Learn and Serve America, Higher Education Program. Santa Monica, CA: RAND.

Hareven, A.(1996). *To Be a Citizen in the Twenty-First Century.* Rajiv Gandhi Institute for Contemporary Studies (New Delhi) Paper No.33

Hunter, Susan (2000) The Impact of Service learning on Democratic and Civic Values. *Political Science and Politics.* September.

James, W. (1910) *The Moral Equivalent of War.* International Conciliation, 27.

Kielsmeier, J.C. (1998). National Service and Service Learning. Partnership for Education Reform. Paper presented at the 4th Global conference on National Youth Service. Windsor Castle, UK.

Putnam, Robert. (1993a). *Making Democracy Work: Civic Traditions in Modern Italy,* Princeton: Princeton University Press.

_____. (1993b). The Prosperous Community: Social Capital and Public Life, " *The American Prospect* 13 (Spring), 35-42.

_____. (2000). *Social Capital and Youth Service.* In: Worldwide Workshop on Youth Involvement as a strategy for Social, Economic, and Democratic Development Proceedings. The Ford Foundation, New York.

Rattanamuk, Supparat. Service-Learning Through Volunteering: The Graduate Volunteer Programme, Thailand," *Voluntary Action. Vol. 5, No.3,* Spring 2003, 54.

SPA (2001) *Proposal*: Regional Training Center for Conflict Management and Social Reconstruction in South East Europe. Society for Psychological Assistance, Zagreb, Croatia.

Walzer, M. (1980) Civility and Civic Virtue in Contemporary America. In: Michael Walzer (Ed.) *Radical Principals.* New York, Basic Books.

10 Practical Steps to Advance National Youth Service

Crick, Bernard. Statement of July 30, 2002 cited by Bill Garland in Country Update from the UK on Youth Community Service, paper presented at the 6th Global Conference on National Youth Service, Buenos Aires, September 2002, p.2.

Federal Ministry of Women Affairs and Youth Development, *Report of the Technical Committee on the Re-Organisation of the National Youth Service Corps (NYSC) Scheme.* Abuja, Nigeria, 2002, viii.

Myers, Lincoln. Interviewed in the *Sunday Guardian Magazine*, Port of Spain, Trinidad & Tobago: November 17, 1991.

Robertson, Paul. Happy to be home again, *Kapiti Observer.* Paraparaumu, New Zealand, June 25, 2001, p 4.

Tapia, Maria Nieves. Service-Learning in Latin America, *Aprender Sirve, Servir Ensena.* Latin America Center for Service-Learning, Buenos Aires, 2002, p. 8

INDEX